SWORD STUDY

Parent Guidebook

Written by
Tammy McMahan

Illustrations by
Doug McGuire

Sword Study
Parent Guidebook

2013 SWORD STUDY PARENT GUIDEBOOK
Copyright © 2013 The Shelby Kennedy Foundation
Published by: The Shelby Kennedy Foundation
First Printing June 2013

Editor, Jill Morris
Design Manager, Caroline McKenzie

ISBN: 978-1-939966-00-1

Dewey Decimal Classification Number: 227

Scripture quotations identified KJV are taken from the King James Version.

Scripture quotations identified NKJV are taken from the New King James Version. Copyright © 1982 by Thomas Nelson, Inc. Used by permission. All rights reserved.

Scripture quotations identified NASB are taken from the The Holy Bible, NEW AMERICAN STANDARD VERSION. Copyright © 1960, 1962, 1968, 1971, 1972, 1973, 1975, 1977, 1995 by The Lockman Foundation. Used by permission. All rights reserved.

Scripture quotations identified NIV are taken from the HOLY BIBLE, NEW INTERNATIONAL VERSION. Copyright © 1973, 1978, 1984 by the International Bible Society. Used by permission of International Bible Society.
All rights reserved.

Scripture quotations identified ESV are taken from The English Standard Version. Copyright © 1993, 1994, 1995, 1996, 2000, 2001, 2002. Used by permission, Crossway Division of Good News Publishers. All rights reserved.

Word Study Part A entries based on Strong's Exhaustive Concordance of the Bible and Greek Dictionary of the New Testament. Word Study Part B entries are based on Vine's Concise Dictionary of the Bible and Zodhiates' Complete Word Study Dictionary: New Testament.

Printed in the United States of America.

For more information about resources for studying the Bible together as a family, or to order additional copies of this resource, visit www.biblebee.org.

~ DEDICATION ~

To the glory of my Heavenly Father.

To my husband Mark, my faithful, loving friend and rock.

To my dear parents, for your faithful example
of walking in the light and abiding in the Word,
and encouraging me to carry on.

~ ACKNOWLEDGEMENTS ~

To... Mom, Caroline, Jill and Susan: you are such a gift as fellow racers.
What an amazing, invigorating, stretching race! Only our Lord knows the details
of the race He set before us. Praise Him for the strength, love, grace and
fellowship that He provided to me through your partnerships. You are the best
fellow racers a friend could ask for... ever! Love you dearly!

To... My dearest prayer warriors and friends: you are mighty, faithful and
enduring. How obviously supernatural to feel your prayers from all
corners of the country and feel as though we have fellowshipped over this
book together. Praise our Lord for His provision of YOU! Love you dearly!

To... Our diligent reviewers, Becky, Dana, Hunter, Kelsey, Kristen, Kristi,
Nicole, Teresa and Tom: may the Lord bless you for your refining words,
efforts and encouragement. Love you dearly!

SECTIONS

SWORD STUDY OVERVIEW

SUMMARY
What to Expect each Week

SWORD STUDY

An in-depth study of 1 John for 5 days each week. The daily study will consist of devotion, investigation of the Scriptures, and guided prayer following the A.C.T.S. model.
Time: approximately 20 minutes

A.C.T.S. PRAYER

A time set aside daily to speak directly to the Lord and write to Him using the A.C.T.S. acrostic prayer model.

FAMILY BONFIRE

A planned gathering time designated for family review and discussion centered around the weekly Sword Study lessons and the unique Bible Bee "Day 10 Diagrams".
Time and day to be determined by family.

BIBLE MEMORY PASSAGES

All family members will be encouraged to memorize the same Bible Memory passages each week. The passages beautifully correspond to what is being studied in the Sword Study. Bible Memory Cards are included at the back of the Parent Guidebook for ease of learning for parents and Young Explorers.

WEEK AT A GLANCE

Weekly

AN INTRODUCTORY STORY

The first day of each week will begin with a vignette. It is designed to be a prelude to the main themes that you will be studying during the week.

FIVE DAYS OF STUDY

Students will be led through five days of study each week. Each book's chapter will be studied over a two-week period, starting with an overview of the chapter and then moving through the Investigative Study to a final "Day 10 Diagram" summary of the entire chapter at the end of the two-week period.

Daily

ON YOUR KNEES: PRAY, WRITE, READ

Students will begin each day by praying for a quiet and focused heart. Then, they will write out verses to create their own copy of Scripture in the WRITE! tab and read through the book.

INVESTIGATIVE STUDY: 1-2-3

Students will be led through simple steps of the Investigative Study by allowing Scripture to answer Scripture.

APPLY!

At the closing of certain days of study, students will apply what they have learned that day. Some days, students are given optional "Digging Deeper" activities to increase their knowledge and understanding.

Continued on next page...

WEEK AT A GLANCE

Daily

A.C.T.S. PRAYER

Each day will conclude with a guided prayer time to help students think through the Scriptures they investigated in their study. Initially, we will help them pray through each step of the A.C.T.S. prayer model. After the first week, we encourage the writing of personal prayers within the Sword Study .

A - Adoration

In Adoration we will worship God for who He is and what He has done. We will focus on His character, attributes, and/or deeds that we saw in His Word that day.

C - Confession

In our time of Confession we will focus on our sin. We will take God's Word, hold it up to our hearts and our lives to see where we miss the mark. You will be led to go before the Lord and confess.

T - Thanksgiving

As we go to the Lord in Thanksgiving, we will express our gratitude to God for who He is and what He has done. We will thank Him for what we have learned about Him that day and for what He has revealed to us in His Word.

S - Supplication

When we approach God in Supplication, we will bring those study-related prayer requests before His throne. Instead of focusing on our circumstances, we will focus on what we have learned in His Word that day and ask Him to help us apply those truths to our lives.

SWORD STUDY VIEWS

1 - THE AERIAL VIEW

From our knees, we will move into our INVESTIGATIVE STUDY of the Bible. Your study begins with the AERIAL VIEW, in which you will read the entire book several times to help you become familiar with the text. This will show you the "lay of the land," like a photo taken from an airplane or a satellite. By researching the author, historical context and original recipients of the book, you will set the stage for more accurate understanding of the text. You will create your own book title that describes the central theme of the book. Your AERIAL VIEW observations will help you build a solid and true foundation for all that you will learn in the upcoming weeks. The AERIAL VIEW will be covered in Week One as we investigate the author, recipient, and the historical context of the book.

2 - THE STREETVIEW

As we continue, we will explore the book from a STREETVIEW perspective, going in for a closer look and focusing in on one chapter at a time. The STREETVIEW involves several exercises. First, you will make general observations of the chapter by looking for exhortations, commands, topics, or lists. Then, you will literally be interviewing the chapter by asking who, what, when, where, why, and how questions. This exercise will be like knocking on someone's door and asking them questions. Next, you will search the chapter for any key words. Finally, from these observations, you will choose a title for the chapter. In addition, as part of the daily INVESTIGATIVE STUDY, you will read through the chapter being studied, making any new or revised observations of the chapter.

3 - UNDER THE RUG

UNDER THE RUG is when we really dig deep to uncover any hidden details. In this step, we will be identifying specific key words and looking up the original Greek words and their meanings. We refer to this step as a "Word Study." We will also look up cross references for the Key Words. These are Scriptures in other parts of the Bible that will provide deeper understanding and context for the Key Word.

APPLY!

APPLY! is where we put it all together – from all the different views – to find what God reveals to us through our study of His Word. This will happen at different levels, depending on where you are in the chapter and on what part of the INVESTIGATIVE STUDY process you are in. Until you finish the UNDER THE RUG level, the *APPLY!* step will pertain in a general way to what you studied that day. Then on the last day of each chapter, you will have an opportunity to summarize through the unique "Day 10 Diagram". Finally, you will be able to apply what you have studied to how you live.

A.C.T.S. PRAYER MODEL

A.C.T.S. PRAYER MODEL

Prayer is key.

Prayer is the expression of our heart towards the Lord and is essential in our one-on-one relationship with Him. Building a regular time of prayer with the Lord is one of the most important things for us to do. We have been given direct access to God Most High. We want to make it a priority.

Prayer is an important work the Lord has given for us to do because He has called us to be His representatives, His agents here on earth. Our prayers can have a huge impact. James 5:16 says, *"The effective prayer of a righteous man can accomplish much"* (NASB). Before Jesus left His disciples, He told them something pretty incredible: *"Truly, truly, I say to you, he who believes in Me, the works that I do shall he do also; and greater works than these shall he do; because I go to the Father. And whatever you ask in My name, that will I do, that the Father may be glorified in the Son. If you ask Me anything in My name, I will do it."* (John 14:12-14 NASB)

Prayer is to be regular and intentional. We want to make the most of what we have been given. You can hear from Paul that we are to be constant and deliberate about prayer: *"With all prayer and petition pray at all times in the Spirit, and with this in view, be on the alert with all perseverance and petition for all the saints"* (Ephesians 6:18 NASB) and *"pray without ceasing."* (1 Thessalonians 5:17 NASB)

If prayer is this important, we want to learn how to pray. The disciples asked Jesus to teach them to pray, and Jesus gave them a model prayer that they could use. We see from this that it is helpful to have a model to go by. It will help us be more effective, efficient, and God-focused in our prayers. So, in the next few pages we will present an easy-to-remember prayer model to use whenever you approach your heavenly Father in prayer. It will help you build a God-centered relationship with the Lord, be deliberate and intentional in prayer, and be a mighty prayer warrior that accomplishes much for the kingdom of God.

A.C.T.S. PRAYER MODEL

A

ADORATION

Adoration is worshiping God for who He is and what He has done. It teaches us to focus specifically on His character, all of His attributes, and His wonderful deeds. It draws attention to His Name. God's Name represents the fullness of everything that God is and does. Take your eyes off of yourself and your circumstances. Fix your eyes upon God the Father, God the Son, and God the Holy Spirit. As you study the book of 1 John and read through various Scriptures, focus on God's character and praise him for it. Focus on who He is. He is your Father, your Almighty God, the LORD!

Let's practice praising God by using His Word, first in 1 Peter and then in Revelation:

1 Peter 1:3-4 (NASB) *Blessed be the God and Father of our Lord Jesus Christ, who according to His great mercy has caused us to be born again to a living hope through the resurrection of Jesus Christ from the dead, 4 to obtain an inheritance which is imperishable and undefiled and will not fade away, reserved in heaven for you,*

"O Lord God, You are the God and Father of our Lord and Saviour Jesus Christ. You are the giver of life. You have caused us to be born again to a living hope. You are our true inheritance."

Revelation 4:8-11 (NASB) *And the four living creatures, each one of them having six wings, are full of eyes around and within; and day and night they do not cease to say, "HOLY, HOLY, HOLY, is THE LORD GOD, THE ALMIGHTY, WHO WAS AND WHO IS AND WHO IS TO COME." 9 And when the living creatures give glory and honour and thanks to Him who sits on the throne, to Him who lives forever and ever, 10 the twenty-four elders will fall down before Him who sits on the throne, and will worship Him who lives forever and ever, and will cast their crowns before the throne, saying,*
11 "Worthy art Thou, our Lord and our God, to receive glory and honour and power; for Thou didst create all things, and because of Thy will they existed, and were created."

"Lord God Almighty, Maker of heaven and earth, You are in control. You sit in heaven and see all that man does. You are the King of kings. You appoint kings and put them in places. You have placed Jesus on Your holy mountain. There is nothing I need to fear for You are God and there is no other."

A.C.T.S. PRAYER MODEL

C

CONFESSION

Confessing your sin is as simple as saying, "God, I did the wrong thing." He wants us to be very specific and say exactly what we thought, said, or did that was not according to His Word. Knowing God's Word is the best way to know what is right and what is wrong. Anytime we know what is right and do not do it, it is sin. But even if we don't know what is right and we do wrong it is sin. So it is best to know God's Word. Lay your heart in your hands and lift it up to God. Confess your fear, your weakness, your grumbling – whatever your sin. During the day, when you sin, confess it immediately.

Let's practice confessing your sin by using God's Word, first in 1 Peter and then in the Psalms:

1 Peter 2:1-3 (NKJV) *Therefore, laying aside all malice, all deceit, hypocrisy, envy, and all evil speaking, 2 as newborn babes, desire the pure milk of the word, that you may grow thereby, 3 if indeed you have tasted that the Lord is gracious.*

"Heavenly Father, I confess that I am prone to wander and I say things that I shouldn't. Please forgive me and renew my heart so that I may desire the pure milk of the Word, that I may grow strong in You."

Psalm 51:1-4 (NKJV) *Have mercy upon me, O God, according to Your lovingkindness; according to the multitude of Your tender mercies, blot out my transgressions. 2 Wash me thoroughly from my iniquity, and cleanse me from my sin. 3 For I acknowledge my transgressions, and my sin is always before me. 4 Against You, You only, have I sinned, and done this evil in Your sight – that You may be found just when You speak, and blameless when You judge.*

David, the psalmist, knows God's loving-kindness and compassion. He openly seeks God's forgiveness for his sin. Do you need to ask God to forgive your hard heart and ask Him to give you a heart like David's? "Lord Jesus, I am so sorry. I do not meditate on your Word day and night. I do not love Your Word like David loves Your Word. Please change my heart." 1 John 1:9 reminds us, *"If we confess our sins, He is faithful and just to forgive us our sins and to cleanse us from all unrighteousness (NKJV)."*

A.C.T.S. PRAYER MODEL

T

THANKSGIVING

Thanksgiving is expressing gratitude to God for who He is and what He has done. Thanksgiving gets personal. It acknowledges that He does not just do mighty deeds – He does mighty deeds for me. It recognizes that God is not just a wonderful God – He is a wonderful God for me. What should we thank God for? Everything! "Rejoice always, pray without ceasing, give thanks in all circumstances; for this is the will of God in Christ Jesus for you" (1 Thessalonians 5:16-18 ESV). This means the hard stuff – even the stuff that is painful and that we might not feel particularly thankful for.

Let's practice thanking God by using His Word, first in 1 Peter and then in the Psalms:

1 Peter 1:8-9 (ESV) *Though you have not seen him, you love him. Though you do not now see him, you believe in him and rejoice with joy that is inexpressible and filled with glory, 9 obtaining the outcome of your faith, the salvation of your souls."*

"Heavenly Father, I rejoice and give great thanks to You. My heart is full of joy and gratefulness for my salvation and all You have done through your Son. Thank You, Jesus. I do love You and believe in You. You have redeemed me, and because of You I am forgiven for my sins. I praise You and I thank You. You are good and You are merciful to give me what I do not deserve."

Psalm 107:1-3 (ESV) *Oh give thanks to the LORD, for he is good, for his steadfast love endures forever! Let the redeemed of the LORD say so, whom he has redeemed from trouble and gathered in from the lands, from the east and from the west, from the north and from the south.*

"Father God, I thank You so much for Your goodness and Your loving-kindness towards me. I thank You that Your loving-kindness is so constant and reliable – it is everlasting and will never fail. You have redeemed me from the clutches of Satan and have gathered me into Your kingdom. You have taken me from a far off land where I was distant from You and gathered me to Yourself. I praise You and thank You for how far You were willing to go to bring me near to You."

A.C.T.S. Prayer Model

S

SUPPLICATION

Supplication is asking God on behalf of others or yourself. When we ask God for help, it nurtures a sense of dependence on Him for everything in our lives. And, since we have so many needs, this will probably be the easiest prayer step for many of us. "And pray in the Spirit on all occasions with all kinds of prayers and requests. With this in mind, be alert and always keep on praying for all the saints" (Ephesians 6:18, NIV). Make a special list of the people God has put in your life and note ways you can lift up their particular needs in prayer.

Supplication is bringing your requests before God on behalf of yourself and others. Let's practice speaking to Him using His Word in 1 Peter:

> 1 Peter 1:13-21 (NIV) *Therefore, prepare your minds for action; be self-controlled; set your hope fully on the grace to be given you when Jesus Christ is revealed. 14 As obedient children, do not conform to the evil desires you had when you lived in ignorance. 15 But just as he who called you is holy, so be holy in all you do; 16 for it is written: "Be holy, because I am holy." 17 Since you call on a Father who judges each man's work impartially, live your lives as strangers here in reverent fear. 18 For you know that it was not with perishable things such as silver or gold that you were redeemed from the empty way of life handed down to you from your forefathers, 19 but with the precious blood of Christ, a lamb without blemish or defect. 20 He was chosen before the creation of the world, but was revealed in these last times for your sake. 21 Through him you believe in God, who raised him from the dead and glorified him, and so your faith and hope are in God.*

"Heavenly Father, help me prepare my mind for action! Help me be self-controlled so that I may set my mind, heart, and energy towards following after You and You alone! I want to be holy as You are holy. Please show me the way. Please mold me and make me. Help me remember that You have bought me with the precious blood of Your Son and my Saviour, Jesus Christ. May I live only to serve You and bring glory to Your name and no other!"

FAMILY BONFIRE

Hear, O Israel: The LORD our God, the LORD is one. You shall love the LORD your God with all your heart and with all your soul and with all your might. And these words that I command you today shall be on your heart. You shall teach them diligently to your children, and shall talk of them when you sit in your house, and when you walk by the way, and when you lie down, and when you rise. You shall bind them as a sign on your hand, and they shall be as frontlets between your eyes. You shall write them on the doorposts of your house and on your gates.

~ Deuteronomy 6:4-9 (ESV) ~

Dear Diligent Parent,

As parents, God has given us the responsibility and privilege of discipling our children to walk with Him through Jesus Christ. Our goal is to come alongside you in that exciting endeavour by providing resources, ideas and encouragement as you shepherd your children, under our perfect Great Shepherd. This is where the Sword Studies and Family Bonfire fit in.

The Sword Study teaches a step by step, in-depth pattern of Bible study for you and your children together. The "Sword Study Overview" will give you and idea of what each week and day will look like.

We highly encourage you to study alongside your children by using the Senior Sword Study, both for your own benefit and personal growth, as well as for an enhanced ability to lead them in their learning and spiritual growth.

It is a time commitment, which will take away from other pursuits. We live busy lives and have an enemy who works hard to distract us in many ways, so it will take a determined effort to keep Christ in the center of our day-to-day lives.

While you could just do the studies as independent family members, we feel that the opportunity to really disciple your children lies in making the time to have a "Family Bonfire" each week.

This is a planned time of family fellowship, intentional discipleship and sharing all that the Lord has taught each of you through the week. It provides mutual encouragement to stay the course, and helps parents to see where and how their children are growing, struggling, learning and asking questions. Of course, some of these benefits can be accomplished spontaneously through day-to-day discussions, but having a planned time makes sure that the busyness of life doesn't swamp the conversation and mutual edification that is so essential to intentional discipleship. Having a set-aside time for fun and spiritual growth as a family also demonstrates to your children what is really important in life.

The rest of this section provides tools to support you in this commitment. We have provided suggestions and a framework on how to accomplish having Family Bonfires each week throughout the summer. They are suggestions and not formulas. You can customize and adapt what we have laid out so that it best suits your family's needs.

We suggest that you hold your Family Bonfire time each weekend, after completing the scheduled five days of the Sword Study.

We have included fun ideas for food and activities to make the Family Bonfires something that everyone anticipates. Additionally, we have provided weekly summaries as snapshots of the content covered in the Sword Studies each week. If some weeks' schedules don't allow you to do the full study yourself, you can still keep up with the kids via these summaries.

The first Family Bonfire of the season will serve as a Kick-Off for the whole study. The following weeks will follow a pattern of opening with prayer, Scripture reading and worship and then family discussion questions. Everyone should bring their Bibles and Sword Studies.

The family discussion questions will include review questions that cover factual knowledge gained from the study and life application questions that draw out the deeper impact of delving into God's Word. On the weeks that contain Day 10 Diagrams, you will review that material. As a parent, be sure to share what God taught you as well.

Always remember to seek God's heart and will during these times. When our hearts and minds are submissive to the Spirit of God, He can do great things. The relationships you are building with each other, with the Lord, and with His Word will be life-long and eternal. The benefit to your family may be far beyond anything you can ask or imagine (Ephesians 3:20).

F A M I L Y   B O N F I R E

S Y L L A B U S

KICK-OFF BONFIRE
Weekend before family begins Sword Study

WEEK 1:   **OVERVIEW**

WEEK 2:   **1 JOHN CHAPTER 1,** *STREETVIEW*

WEEK 3:   **1 JOHN CHAPTER 1,** *UNDER THE RUG*
Day 10 Diagram

WEEK 4:   **1 JOHN CHAPTER 2,** *STREETVIEW*

WEEK 5:   **1 JOHN CHAPTER 2,** *UNDER THE RUG*
Day 10 Diagram

WEEK 6:   **1 JOHN CHAPTER 3,** *STREETVIEW*

WEEK 7:   **1 JOHN CHAPTER 3,** *UNDER THE RUG*
Day 10 Diagram

WEEK 8:   **1 JOHN CHAPTER 4,** *STREETVIEW*

WEEK 9:   **1 JOHN CHAPTER 4,** *UNDER THE RUG*
Day 10 Diagram

WEEK 10:   **1 JOHN CHAPTER 5,** *STREETVIEW*

WEEK 11:   **1 JOHN CHAPTER 5,** *UNDER THE RUG*
Day 10 Diagram

WEEK 12:   **REVIEW**

K I C K - O F F   B O N F I R E

"Get Ready!"

Prepare: Read through your Parent Guidebook Sword Study Overview, A.C.T.S. Prayer Model and Family Bonfire Sections. Bring a calendar and your Parent Guidebook. Have all of your family members bring their Sword Studies, Bibles and Bible Memory Cards. The purpose of the Kick-Off Bonfire is to get your family prepared and excited for a summer in God's Word through the Sword Studies.

One practical step to accomplish before or during your first Bonfire is to organize your family's Bible Memory Cards. You may want to mark each child's cards with their initials, or with a certain color of marker or sticker. Some find it helpful to hole-punch a corner of the cards and store them on a ring for ease of use.

We have provided a suggested syllabus for your planning purposes. Either ahead of time, or together at the Family Bonfire, plan the dates for all of your Bonfires. Do you have a vacation planned? Can you have a special Bonfire there, or make adjustments on the week that you come back home? Does Dad have a business trip? Perhaps you could still hold a Bonfire with the use of Skype. The point is to have a plan ahead of time, so that your time together for the Family Bonfire is not buried under the normal busyness of life.

Creative Family Ideas for Kick-Off Bonfire – Theme, "On Your Mark, Get Set, Go!"
• Each week in this part of your Family Bonfire area, we will give you several ideas to add fun to your weekend that also ties into the theme of the week's Sword Study lessons and Bible Memory recommendation.
• For your weekly "Bonfire," find a comfortable spot for your whole family to gather. You may want to have a special meal, snacks or even a campfire, if you have the facilities. Cultivate the atmosphere for a fun family gathering, a "family party night" that everyone looks forward to all week.
• After this "Get Ready!" section, each week the next page will give a suggested outline for a Family Bonfire that corresponds with the material and study of the specific week's lessons. Again, this is not meant to be a formula, only a launching pad for what works for your family.
• Hide a small treasure for each child or one family item. Allow everyone to go find their treasure using simple clues. Gather back at your Bonfire and talk about how God's Word is a hidden treasure to us. Discuss the importance of spending time studying the Bible as you kick-off your Sword Study.
• Plan a special dinner at a local Turkish restaurant to highlight the start of your family time in 1 John. Discuss how John would have been in Ephesus and note the atmosphere of the restaurant.
• Find or print off a map of modern day Turkey. Bring it to your Bonfire with a globe to help your family have a good understanding of where John was located as he wrote 1 John.

F A M I L Y   B O N F I R E

KICK-OFF BONFIRE SCHEDULE

Begin with Prayer

Worship:

Sing hymns and/or songs focused on the Lord's attributes.
Have your children look through their Bible Memory Cards and share a passage that they already know.

Read Scripture:

Psalm 111 *(Divide the chapter and have each family member read a few verses.)*

Family Discussion Questions:

What is the theme of Psalm 111?
(Praising the Lord; verse 1 and 10)

How are we to praise the Lord?
(We are to praise the Lord with all of our hearts, according to verse 1.)

What is done with all the works of the Lord?
(According to verse 2, the works of the Lord are sought out, studied and pondered by those who have pleasure and delight in them.)

Have each of you organized a special place to do your Bible Study?

Do you have any concerns about starting your Sword Study that we can all pray for this week?

Bible Memory Recommendation (for upcoming week):

Psalm 111:10, Jeremiah 9:23-24

Close: Read Psalm 111:10 and Jeremiah 9:23-24 to your family. May these passages be an encouagement to your family as you choose to seek understanding and knowledge of God through His Word as a family!

Close in prayer as a family by going around the circle, first in Adoration, then Confession, then Thanksgiving, and concluding with Supplication.

W E E K   O N E

"GET READY!"

Prepare: Complete the Senior Sword Study Week 1 **OR** read 1 John.

Quick Notes: The Sword Study students completed Week 1 by observing the book of 1 John from an AERIAL VIEW. Each day they began with prayer and a time of writing cross reference Scriptures that encouraged them to gain wisdom through the study of God's Word. During the inductive study portion, they studied the author by looking at various Scriptures throughout the Bible and investigated the false teaching of John's day, Gnosticism, for an understanding of the historical context of 1 John. To close the week, on Day 5 the students were asked to title, summarize and choose a key verse for each chapter from their initial observations of 1 John. After the study section each day, they were encouraged to pray using the A.C.T.S. prayer model.

Summary: 1 John was a letter written by John, a close friend of Jesus, to the Christians who were being troubled by the false teachings of the Gnostic teachers. John had left his occupation as a fisherman to become a disciple of Christ. Although he was known as a "Son of Thunder" for his dynamic personality, this letter has a gentle, fatherly tone throughout the chapters. John repetitively shares his reasons for writing this letter to the body of Christ. His style is one of circling by repetition and zeroing in on his main purposes of assuring and encouraging his readers of their salvation through Jesus and fellowship with the Father, Son and other believers. John's words thunder through history to us as current day students of the Word: "God is light! God is love! Beloved children of God, love Him with all your hearts, minds and souls! Walk in His light!"

Creative Family Ideas for the weekend – Theme: "Getting to know John"

• Take your family fishing. Pack your lunch and enjoy the day at the lake or pond. For the super-adventurous, bring materials for a campfire and plan to eat your catch. Make sure to have some "Plan B" items in case the fish aren't biting! There are lots of good talking points around fishing...

• Purchase a children's game of "Let's Go Fishing." Or, have a craft day making a set of your own pretend fishing set with dowel rods, string, paper, markers and lamination pages from your local craft or super store. Play the game at your Family Bonfire; regardless of the ages of your children, everyone can have fun playing. To make it even more exciting, use a children's pool as the pond.

• Play "Follow the Leader" or "Mother May I?" and then explain how being a disciple is following Jesus, and how He lived and cared for others.

• Watch a historical speech and discuss how the speaker is dynamic and resembles "thunder." Make the correlation between the speaker and how John was named by Jesus in Mark 3:16-18. Speech possibilities could include: Martin Luther's "I Have a Dream," John F. Kennedy's 1961 Inaugural Address ("Ask not what your country can do…"), or an apologetic presentation by Ray Comfort, Billy Graham, John Stonestreet, Del Tackett or Ravi Zacharias.

F A M I L Y   B O N F I R E

W E E K   O N E

Begin with Prayer

Read Scripture:
>   Read Matthew 4:17-25 and Psalm 29

Worship:

>   Sing "I Will Follow" by Chris Tomlin, hymns (such as "As The Deer") and/or other worship songs.
>   Share memorized verses

Family Discussion Questions:
>   **Who was the author of 1 John?**
>   *(John, the son of Zebedee)*
>
>   **What did you learn about the author?**
>   *(Fisherman, Son of Zebedee, Brother to James, Matthew 4:17-24; Disciple of Jesus Christ, Matthew 10:1-2; Present with Jesus during transfiguration, Mark 9:1-2; Part of Jesus' inner circle, close friend, Mark 14:31-41; Prisoner on Patmos and Bondservant of God, Revelation 1:1, 9-11)*
>
>   **What philosophy were the false prophets teaching during the time of John's letter?**
>   *(Gnosticism)*
>
>   **Describe Gnosticism.**
>   *(Answers will vary in depth. General definition of Gnosticism is "a teaching that depended on knowledge as the end-all of salvation." Gnostic teachers believed God was only a spirit, and that Jesus either did not come to earth or was not God.)*
>
>   **Have each family member share their chapter titles for the five chapters of 1 John.**
>   *(Answers will vary)*
>
>   **Ask if anyone has a personal prayer need that the rest of the family can pray for this week.**

Bible Memory Recommendation (for upcoming week):
>   John 8:12, John 17:3

Close:
>   Read John 8:12 and John 17:3.
>   Close in prayer as a family by going around the circle, first in Adoration, then Confession, then Thanksgiving, and concluding with Supplication.

W E E K   T W O

"GET READY!"

Prepare: Complete the Senior Sword Study Week 2 **OR** read 1 John.

Write: Your children have started writing the book of 1 John. They have written out the text of 1 John 1:1-6. Using the "My Copy of 1 John" section in your Sword Study Parent Guidebook, catch up to them by writing these six verses of 1 John 1.

Quick Notes: The Sword Study students lowered their perspective's view from the big picture to a more detailed look at 1 John 1 this week. All levels began by interviewing the chapter. While the younger learners took two days to accomplish the interview exercise, the Junior and Senior Sword Study students gathered lists, exhortations and comparisons from 1 John 1. During Days 3 and 4, they looked at specific phrases in 1 John in light of other passages scattered throughout Scripture to gain a better background understanding. Everyone closed the week learning about the word study process in preparation for next week's UNDER THE RUG level.

Summary: John jumped right into his letter to the church without a self-introduction or greetings. He immediately declares his witness of Jesus' presence on the earth, in the flesh. Declaring that he had seen, heard and witnessed Jesus himself, John makes his case as a knowledgeable preacher of the truth to us, as well as to those confused by Gnosticism's claims. Next, he shares that the message he and the other disciples heard from Jesus was that God is light and there is no darkness in Him. True believers walk in the light, fellowship with one another and have salvation through Jesus' blood. We chose 1 John 1:3 as the key verse.

Creative Family Ideas for the weekend – Theme: "Light"
• Play a game of flashlight tag with your family.
• Investigate nocturnal animals. How do they see so well in the dark?
• Play "Hide & Seek" with glow-in-the-dark bracelets- hide around a room or your whole house!
• Have your Family Bonfire by candlelight or flashlight.
• Using glow-in-the-dark paint, create poster board signs. Place them all around a room with passages. Or create a treasure hunt using the signs. Leave them turned around until after your Family Bonfire, then turn off the lights and begin your hunt.
• Discuss how everyone feels when they are in the dark. What happens when you walk around in the dark? Pair off in two's and take turns walking around blind-folded without assistance. (The partners without the blind folds make sure that no one gets hurt!)

W E E K   T W O

Begin with Prayer

Read Scripture:

Read Psalm 27 and 1 Peter 2:9-12

Worship:

Sing "10,000 Reasons" by Matt Redman, or sing other hymns or worship songs

Share memorized verses

Family Discussion Questions:

What name did John call Jesus in the beginning of his letter?

(Word of Life; 1 John 1:1)

Name the ways John claimed to have witnessed Jesus on earth, in the flesh.

(John saw, heard, touched and walked with Jesus while he was a man on earth, 1 John 1:1)

John made two comparisons in 1 John 1; he compared light with _____ and truth with _____?

(Light to darkness, 1 John 1:5 and truth to lie, 1 John 1:6)

Turn to your Week 2 Day 3 investigative study and share something that you learned about one of John's phrases.

(Answers will vary.)

Ask if anyone has a personal prayer need that the rest of the family can pray for this week.

Bible Memory Recommendation (for upcoming week):

1 John 1:3, 1 John 1:9

Close:

Read 1 John 1:3 and 9.

Close in prayer as a family by going around the circle, first in Adoration, then Confession, then Thanksgiving, and concluding with Supplication.

F A M I L Y   B O N F I R E

W E E K   T H R E E

"GET READY!"

Prepare: Complete the Senior Sword Study Week 3 **OR** read 1 John.

Write: Write verses 7 through 10 of 1 John 1 in your "Write!" section of the Parent Guidebook. Using the symbols below, mark any references to God that you find in Chapter 1.

God the Father   God the Son   God the Holy Spirit

Quick Notes: Students finished their spotlight on 1 John 1 this week. They did this through the UNDER THE RUG activities of word studies and cross referencing. We chose *fellowship* and *sin* as the two Key Words for Chapter 1. They learned the Greek words, their transliterations and definitions. Next, they investigated passages outside of 1 John that used *fellowship* and *sin*. Everyone was introduced to their first Day 10 Diagram on Day 5, which is a pictorial summary of 1 John 1.

Summary: God is Light and He does not fellowship in the darkness. It is only through His Son, Jesus, that He can have a relationship with us and see us without sin. As a result of the event we call "salvation," He looks at us, sees us wrapped in Jesus' righteousness, and accepts us as His adopted children; otherwise, He sees us wrapped in our sin and, as a perfect God, cannot enter into a relationship with us. If we have trusted Jesus as our payment for sin, we have the seed of Christ, the Holy Spirit, dwelling in us. Then, we have not only been saved from the penalty of sin, which is death, but have victorious power over sin's bondage and are able to walk in the Light.

Creative Family Ideas for the weekend – Theme: "Fellowship"

• Plan a progressive fellowship dinner with like-minded friends next week. Create the invitations, brainstorm and plan as a family at this week's Bonfire. Be sure to plan for time to talk about all the Lord is doing!

• Gather the materials to create friendship bracelets.

• Either do or show one another your Day 10 Diagrams of 1 John 1.

• Join with another family for your Bonfire time.

WEEK THREE

Begin with Prayer

Read Scripture:

Read Acts 2:42-47 and Philippians 2:1-7

Worship:

Sing or listen to "Power of the Cross" by the Gettys, sing hymns or other songs
Share memorized verses

Family Discussion Questions:

Since one of your word studies was about fellowship, describe what you learned about fellowship this week.
(Various answers. General, paraphrased definition of Christian fellowship is "gathering of like-minded Believers to pray, hear preaching or worship God.")

What is sin?
(An action against God's rules)

Who has sinned?
(Everyone has sinned, Romans 3:23)

Before we can fellowship with God, we must have a relationship. How do we get a relationship with God?
(We must confess with our mouth that Jesus is Lord and believe He was raised from the dead, Romans 10:9-10)

What does sin do to our fellowship with God?
(Sin breaks our fellowship with God. He wants us to confess our sin to restore fellowship, 1 John 1:9)

Review the "Day 10 Diagram" and ask if there are any questions. Ask each family member to share his or her diagram.
(A completed Diagram is on the next page for your reference. Often, children are excited to share their colored creations!)

Ask if anyone has a personal prayer need that the rest of the family can pray for this week.

Bible Memory Recommendation (for upcoming week):

Job 15:14-16, Proverbs 28:13-14

Close: Read Psalm 130. Close in prayer as a family by going around the circle first in
Adoration, then Confession, then Thanksgiving, and concluding with Supplication.

Title: **Walk in the Light!**
Key Verse: 1 John 1:3

Chapter: **One**
♥ :Psalms 111:10, Jeremiah 9:23-24
John 8:12, John 17:3
1 John 1:3, 1 John 1:9

Greek Words: Fellowship & Sin

〜 Koinonia:
Partnership, Fellow Traveler

〜 Hamartano/Hamartia:
To Trespass/An Offense

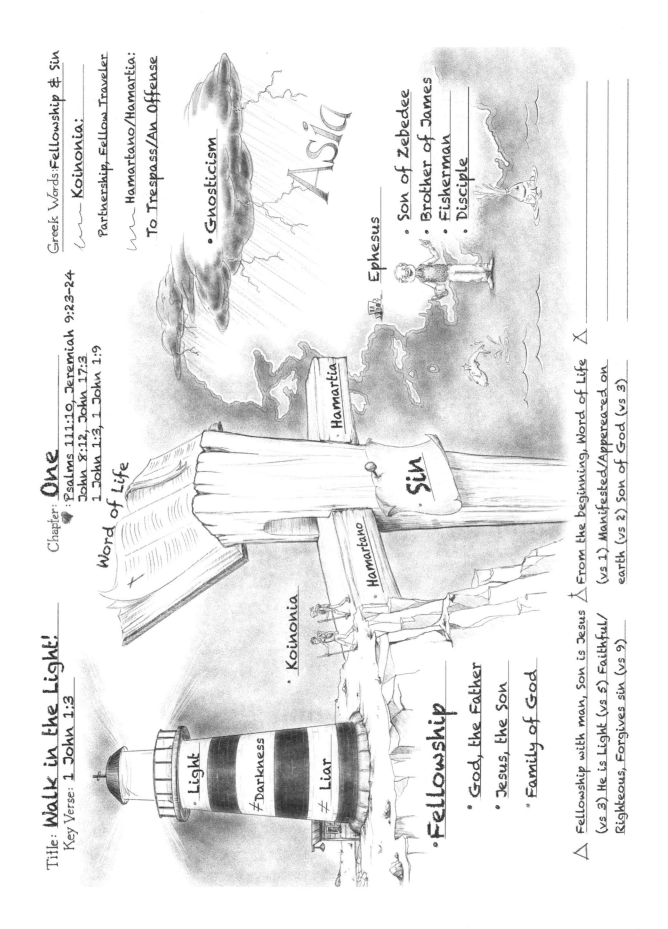

• Gnosticism

Asia

Ephesus

• Son of Zebedee
• Brother of James
• Fisherman
• Disciple

Word of Life

Hamartia

• Sin

Hamartano

• Koinonia

Light
≠ Darkness
≠ Liar

• **Fellowship**
• God, the Father
• Jesus, the Son
• Family of God

△ Fellowship with man, Son is Jesus △ From the beginning, Word of Life Χ
(vs 3) He is Light (vs 5) Faithful/   (vs 1) Manifested/Appeareed on
Righteous, Forgives sin (vs 9)   earth (vs 2) Son of God (vs 3)

W E E K F O U R

"GET READY!"

Prepare: Complete the Senior Sword Study Week 4 **OR** read 1 John and Chapter 2 twice.

Write: To keep in step with your children's investigation of 1 John 2, write verses 1-16 in your Parent Guidebook.

Quick Notes: During the first two days of Week 4 your explorers focused on 1 John 2 by writing short, summary phrases of the 29 verses of this chapter. John repeated the phrases, "I write" and "I have written." On Day 3, everyone noted his reasons for writing. The Senior and Junior Sword Studies highlighted the many "If-Then" statements on Day 4. Everyone wrapped up their STREETVIEW of 1 John 2 by looking at John's exhortations, unfamiliar words and choosing Key Words.

Summary: John addresses his readers: fathers, young men, children. Each of the titles John uses portrays a fatherly term of endearment. There is no doubt that the once "Son of Thunder" has softened a bit and is displaying fatherly love to his children in the faith. In this chapter, John gives "his children" assurance of their status in Christ and resulting eternal life. An exhortation not to love the things of the world is particularly poignant to his audience both in the past and present. We chose 1 John 2:13 as the key verse.

Creative Family Ideas for the weekend – Theme: "The World"
• Use this week's lesson as an opportunity to weed through your family's belongings for things that are unused and donate them to a good cause.
• Play a family game of Monopoly. Talk about how easy it is to get excited about money and property!
• Take a week's fast from sports, television, or technology.
• Calculate the cost of your family attending an event, and dontate the cost to a ministry.

WEEK FOUR

Begin with Prayer

Read Scripture:
> Read Isaiah 46:5-13 and Psalm 90

Worship:
> Sing hymns and/or worship songs
> Share memorized verses

Family Discussion Questions:

What is an "advocate?"
(A person who pleads the case of another.)

Who is our Advocate?
(Jesus is our Advocate.,1 John 2:1)

What is "propitiation?"
(Payment for a debt)

Why do we need propitiation from God?
(To pay the debt for our sin, 1 John 2:2)

What are some of the titles that John used for his recipients in 1 John 2?
(Little children, verse 1; Fathers, verse 13; Young men, verse 13; Children, verse 18)

What three exhortations/commands did John give in Chapter 2?
(Day 5: Do not love the world, nor things in it, verse 15; Abide in what you heard in the beginning, verse 24; Abide in Jesus, verse 28.)

Ask if anyone has a personal prayer need that the rest of the family can pray for this week.

Bible Memory Recommendation (for the upcoming week):
> Psalm 36:7-10, John 8:31-32

Close:
> Read Psalm 36:7-10 and John 8:31-32.
> Close in prayer as a family by going around the circle, first in Adoration, then Confession, then Thanksgiving, and concluding with Supplication.

W E E K   F I V E

"GET READY!"

Prepare: Complete the Senior Sword Study Week 5 **OR** read 1 John.

Write: Your children have finished writing 1 John, Chapter 2; you can do the same in your "Write!" pages. Mark any references to God.

Quick Notes: "I *know* the President because I <u>saw</u> his picture in the newspaper."
"I *know* the President because I was his <u>personal</u> assistant for 10 years."

In the small letter of 1 John, there are 30 occurrences of two different Greek words both of which are translated "know" in English. Students learned the first Greek word, *eido*, means a surface knowledge of someone or something, similar to "see" or "perceive." The second, *ginosko*, means to have a growing, deepening personal knowledge of someone. How amazing to watch John effectively use these two words to show us the differences between true Christianity and the false teaching of the Gnostics! They also studied the Greek word for *abide*, meaning "to remain, dwell or live with another in heart, mind and will" or "to remain steadfast." After studying each word, each level took deeper looks by cross referencing various passages with the words *know* and *abide*.

Summary: John emphasized the importance of the different levels of knowledge. There would be many that said they knew God, but only those who *abided* by His ways were truly of Him. John gave pointers on how to evaluate one's true identity. Did they love their brother? Were they walking in the light? Have they remained with us? Carefully, in fatherly love, he assured them that they *know* Jesus and the word of God *abides* in them. We chose verse 13 as the key verse.

Creative Family Ideas for the weekend – Theme: "Abide"
• Play games that make family members stick together (abide), such as three-legged races or wheelbarrow races.
• Find the retro game of "Password" or create your own game of synonyms to play during your Bonfire.
• Build a fort and abide in it all day long with your younger crew. Plan to have the whole family attend dinner with you at the end of the day.
• Create popsicle stick houses and discuss how we are to dwell in Jesus' ways.
• Practice your week's Bible Memory passages by putting each word on a different piece of paper- mix them up and have family members race to put them in order.
• Enlarge your "Day 10 Diagram" to poster size or bigger for a group coloring activity at your Family Bonfire. (You have our permission to make one enlarged copy for your family!)
• Consider purchasing "The Hiding Place" in preparation for Week 8 or 9's Bonfire.

WEEK FIVE

Begin with Prayer

Read Scripture:
Read John 15:1-15

Worship:
Sing "He is the Vine & we are the branches….His banner over me is love!," hymns and/or songs
Share memorized verses

Family Discussion Questions:

Who is the vine? Who are the branches?
(Jesus is the vine, John 15:1) (Christians are the branches, John 15:2)

What does the word *abide* mean?
(To dwell, live, remain with another in mind, heart and will)

What happens when we *abide* with the vine?
(We have fruit that shows we are abiding in Jesus. We look like Him! John 15:2)

Who *abides* in our hearts?
(The Spirit of God, our Helper, Galatians 4:6)

What are the two meanings for *know* as John uses it in his letter?
(A casual knowledge like an acquaintance and a deep, intimate knowledge like a best friend.)

Review the "Day 10 Diagram". Ask each family member to share his or her diagram. (A completed Diagram is on the next page for your reference.)

Ask if anyone has a personal prayer need that the rest of the family can pray for this week.

Bible Memory Recommendation (for upcoming week):
2 Corinthians 6:16-18, Isaiah 43:1-2

Close:
Read 2 Corinthians 6:16-18 and Isaiah 43:1-2.
Close in prayer as a family by going around the circle, first in Adoration, then Confession, then Thanksgiving, and concluding with Supplication.

Title: You Know God!

Key Verse: 1 John 2:1,3

Chapter: Two

Greek Words: Know & Abide

Eido: Aquainted, See

Ginosko: Deeply, Process

Meno: Dwell, Remain
in heart, mind & spirit

♥ : Job 15:14-16,
Proverbs 28:13-14,
Psalm 36:7-10,
John 8:31-32

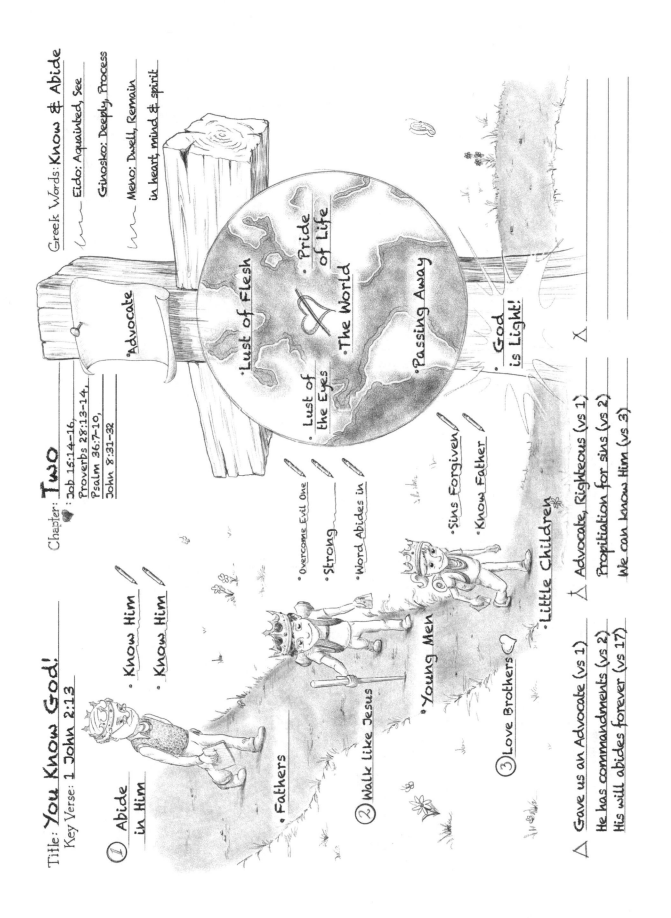

① Abide
___ in Him

• Know Him
• Know Him

• Fathers ___

• Advocate

• Lust of Flesh
• Pride
   of Life
• The World
• Lust of
  the Eyes
• Passing Away

• God
  is Light!

• Overcome Evil One
• Strong ___
• Word Abides in

② Walk like Jesus
• Young Men ___

• Sins Forgiven!
• Know Father ___

• Love Brothers
• Little Children

③ Love Brothers ___

△ Advocate, Righteous (vs 1)
Propitiation for sins (vs 2)
We can know Him (vs 3)

△ Gave us an Advocate (vs 1)
He has commandments (vs 2)
His will abides forever (vs 17)

W E E K   S I X

"GET READY!"

Prepare: Complete the Senior Sword Study Week 6 **OR** read 1 John and read Chapter 3 a second time.

Write: Begin writing 1 John 3 by copying verses 1 through 12.

Quick Notes: 1 John, Chapter 3 became the new focus this past week. The first days' assignment turned the tables on the students and made them ask questions of the chapter's verses. They spent the remainder of the week comparing the difference between the children of God and the children of the devil. John used Cain as an example of darkness, so on Day 5, everyone turned to Genesis to understand his story.

Summary: Chapter 3 begins with John describing the love of God as being so great that He gives us the right to be called children of God. He dwells on the attributes of God's children and then contrasts them to the behaviors of those who belong to the enemy of God, the devil. John once again takes the opportunity to present the gospel by highlighting our adoption into God's family through Jesus. We are not second-rate citizens, but full, birthright children of the Kingdom of Heaven.

Creative Family Ideas for the weekend – Theme: "Children of the King"

• Visit Steven Curtis Chapman's website, www.showhope.com, to learn more about adoption.
• Make crowns for whole family to wear at Family Bonfire.
• Create and act out a play about Esther.
• Watch the Veggie Tales *Queen Esther* movie.
• Ask your children who they have been praying for from Week 6, Day 4's Apply.
• Read a book or watch a DVD about Billy Graham.

W E E K   S I X

Begin with Prayer

Read Scripture:
Read Psalm 145:1-10 and Psalm 150:4-6

Worship:
Sing hymns and/or worship songs
Share memorized verses

Family Discussion Questions:
Because God loves us so much, what does He call us?
(His children, 1 John 3:1)

What are the two groups of children?
(Children of God and children of the devil, 1 John 3:10)

What are the children of God supposed to practice?
(The children of God practice righteousness, 1 John 3:10)

How are the children of God supposed to love?
(They are to love in word and deed, 1 John 3:18)

Who is the Old Testament example used in 1 John Chapter 3?
(Cain, the evil one, 1 John 3:12; Various answers, see Genesis 4:1-16)

Ask if anyone has a personal prayer need that the rest of the family can pray for this week.

Bible Memory Recommendation (for upcoming week):
2 Corinthians 5:20-21, Isaiah 45:22-23

Close:
Read 2 Corinthians 5:20-21 and Isaiah 45:22-23.
Close in prayer as a family by going around the circle, first in Adoration, then Confession, then Thanksgiving, and concluding with Supplication.

W E E K   S E V E N

"GET READY!"

Prepare: Complete the Senior Sword Study Week 7 **OR** read 1 John.

Write: Week 7 finished the in-depth look of 1 John 3; write the remaining verses in your Parent Guidebook. Mark any references to God in the chapter.

Quick Notes: Word studies of *righteous* and *righteousness* were the tasks of Week 7 for all levels. The children learned the details surrounding those that live in righteousness and were deemed righteous. Heroes of the faith, according to the Word of God, are those who walk in righteousness…in God's ways. The greatest example, of course, was Jesus. The youth investigated the lifestyles of the righteous examples and spent a day looking specifically at Jesus' life.

Summary: John emphasized the life of the children of God as being characterized by righteous living. They look different than those serving themselves and the enemy. God's children follow His commands, love one another and do not practice sin. The old adage of "practicing what you preach" comes from the 1 John 3:18 passage exhorting the children of God to love in word and deed. We will watch John zero in on this passage's message when we move into Chapter 4. We chose 1 John 3:1 as the key verse.

Creative Family Ideas for the weekend – Theme, "The righteous, holy and faithful… Heroes of the Faith"

• Bring your family to a fun, putt-putt golf course. At the conclusion of your game, announce the winner and then ask everyone if they realize the difference between these holes and the definition of holy. Use the opportunity to talk about the righteousness of God.

• Read a biography or watch a biographical DVD or a Heroes of the Faith DVD.

• Assign each member of the family a Hebrews 11 "Hero of the Faith" and have them act out a short skit.

• Play a game of charades using all heroes of the faith.

F A M I L Y   B O N F I R E

W E E K   S E V E N

Begin with Prayer

Read Scripture:
Read Hebrews 11:1-40 and Matthew 5:14-16.

Worship:
Sing hymns and/or worship songs
Share memorized verses

Family Discussion Questions:
<u>Review time!</u>
What type of writing is 1 John? *(Letter)*
What name did John call Jesus in the beginning of his letter? *(Word of Life, 1 John 1:1)*
What were the false teachers teaching? *(Gnosticism)*
Who has sinned? *(Everyone has sinned, Romans 3:23)*
Who is our Advocate? *(Jesus is our Advocate, 1 John 2:1)*
What is propitiation? *(Payment for a debt)*
What does the word *abide* mean? *(To dwell, live, remain with another in mind, heart and will)*

What is the definition of *righteous*?
(Doing what is right according to God's rules. God is the only One who is righteous without failure.)

The righteous children are busy, right? Name a few examples of righteous men you learned about.
(Answers will vary: Noah, Abraham, Cornelius, Simeon and Jesus are among those that were investigated.)

Review the "Day 10 Diagram" and ask if there are any questions. Ask each family member to share his or her diagram.
(A completed Diagram is on the next page for your reference.)

Ask if anyone has a personal prayer need that the rest of the family can pray for this week.

Bible Memory Recommendation (for upcoming week):
1 John 4:7-10, Philippians 3:8-11

Close: Read 1 John 4:7-10 and Philippians 3:8-11. Close in prayer as a family by going around the circle first, in Adoration, then Confession, then Thanksgiving, and concluding with Supplication.

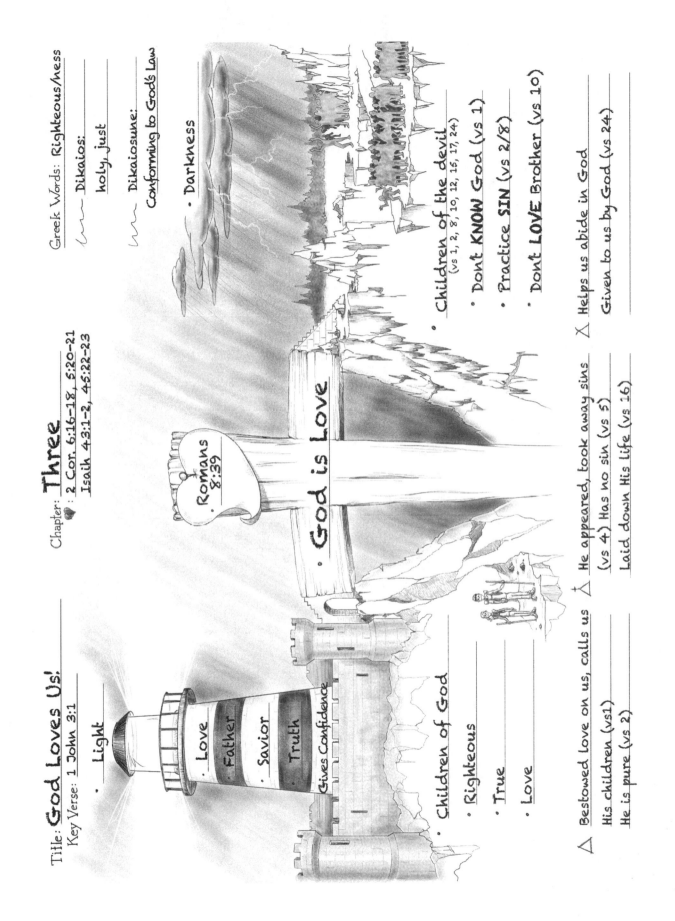

Title: **God Loves Us!**
Key Verse: 1 John 3:1

Chapter: **Three**
• 2 Cor 6:16-18, 5:20-21
  Isaih 43:1-2, 46:22-23

Greek Words: Righteous/ness
Dikaios: holy, just
Dikaiosune: Conforming to God's Law

• Light

Love · Father · Savior · Truth
Gives Confidence

Children of God
• Righteous
• True
• Love

Romans 8:39

God is Love

• Darkness

Children of the devil (vs 1, 2, 8, 10, 12, 15, 17, 24)
• Don't **KNOW** God (vs 1)
• Practice **SIN** (vs 2/8)
• Don't **LOVE** Brother (vs 10)

△ Bestowed love on us, calls us
His children (vs1)
He is pure (vs 2)

△ He appeared, took away sins
(vs 4) Has no sin (vs 5)
Laid down His life (vs 16)

X Helps us abide in God
Given to us by God (vs 24)

W E E K   E I G H T

"GET READY!"

Prepare: Complete Senior Sword Study Week 8 **OR** read 1 John and read Chapter 4 twice.

Write: Your children have been writing 1 John 4. They have reached verse 9 in their "Write!" pages. You will need to do the same to keep up with them!

Quick Notes: Students moved to 1 John 4 this week. They spent four days questioning and cross referencing phrases from Chapter 4. They summarized the gospel in their own words, with their own story, by using 1 John 4:4, 9 and 10 as they closed the week in Day 5. This week prepared students for next week's in-depth look at God's type of love by setting the stage of John's call to love the Lord our God with all our hearts, minds and wills above all. As a result, we are to love one another as well.

Summary: John describes the evidence of a child of God as his or her example of following God's commandments. The first commandment was to love the Lord with all their beings. The second was to love one another. These actions would show their association with Jesus. This fourth chapter of 1 John is all about love; the love God has for us, the love we have for Him and the love we are to have towards others. This is no ordinary love.

Creative Family Ideas for the weekend – Theme: "Commands"

• Bring back the basics of commands this week in your Family Bonfire! Play a game of "Mother May I?" or "Simon Says" or "Red light, Green light."
• Watch the classic movie, "The Ten Commandments," with popcorn and treats.
• Check out Geo-Caching. This is a free app that has millions of treasure hunts around the country. There is even one for the Sword Study, called "Sword Study Treasure." Talk about how following directions is the key to any successful hunt.
• Print out directions to a favorite park. Don't disclose your destination, and have one of your children be the co-pilot. Your co-pilot reads the map directions out loud to get you to the park. Have a picnic lunch there to celebrate.
• Set up a fun obstacle course. Make it complex. Begin by giving everyone three short directions, such as: "Run around the tree," "Jump over the stick," "Skip back to me." Add a new direction and do it again. Once you get to six tasks, consider pairing your family up to work at accomplishing the goal with two people's brain power!
• Search the internet for "Fun Following Directions Games." There are lots of great games for all ages!
• Watch "The Hiding Place" this week or next.

W E E K E I G H T

Begin with Prayer

Read Scripture:
Read Nehemiah 1:5, Matthew 22:37-38 and John 13:35.

Worship:
Sing hymns and/or worship songs
Share memorized verses

Family Discussion Questions:

What is a command?
(A direction or order)

Who loved first? Did God love us, or did we love God?
(God loved us first, 1 John 4:19)

What did God do because of His love for us, according to 1 John 4:9-10?
(God sent His son to be a payment, propitiation, for our sins.)

Why should we love other people?
(God loved us so we should love others, 1 John 4:11)

Ask if anyone has a personal prayer need that the rest of the family can pray for this week.

Bible Memory Recommendation (for upcoming week):
2 Corinthians 5:14-15, Ephesians 5:1-4

Close:
Read 2 Corinthians 5:14-15 and Ephesians 5:1-4.
Close in prayer as a family by going around the circle, first in Adoration, then Confession, then Thanksgiving, and concluding with Supplication.

W E E K N I N E

"GET READY!"

Prepare: Complete the Senior Sword Study Week 9 **OR** read 1 John 4.

Write: Finish writing 1 John 4 in your "My Copy of 1 John" section and mark any references to God in Chapter 4.

Quick Notes: **Love**. God's love was the one and only focus for Week 9 of the 1 John Sword Study. Students looked at the four Greek words that represent *love*. Agape *love* is the *love* that John uses over and over in this small letter. Everyone marked the word *love* throughout the book with either a red colored pencil or a heart symbol.

Summary: 1 John 4 relays a crucial truth regarding love. The Greek word for God's love is *agape*. This type of love is different from all the others in that it is a compassionate, unconditional love. God's love is self-sacrificing versus a "when I feel like it" emotion, physical affection or friendship. This love is from the perspective of the giver displaying what is needed by the recipient. Thus, we see God, the Father, giving His Son as a payment for man's sins while man was still a sinner, an enemy. God's love saved us sacrificially. Now, through His power, He calls us to love others in the same manner, which will result in the world seeing Him. Thus, we chose 1 John 4:10 as the key verse.

Creative Family Ideas for the weekend – Theme: "Love"

• Bring supplies to create anonymous "love" notes to family and friends. Mail your cards after your Family Bonfire!

• Show your family's love to another family by coming up with a special gift of love. Bake a meal, clean a house or care for a lawn as a family.

• Bake bread for the elderly.

• Offer to care for the children of another family. Give the parents a gift card for dinner and send them on a date night.

• Regardless of the month, have a Valentine's Party!

• As a family, place old pennies, one per family member, in vinegar at this week's Family Bonfire in preparation for your Week 10 Bonfire.

• Consider purchasing the DVD, "St. John in Exile" with Dean Jones.

W E E K   N I N E

Begin with Prayer

Read Scripture:
Read 1 Corinthians 13

Worship:
Sing hymns and/or worship songs
Share memorized verses

Family Discussion Questions:

What is phileo love?
(Brotherly, friendship love)

What is agape love?
(God-like love that is of the will, self-sacrificing, compassionate and unconditional)

What did God's love do for us?
(Sent His Son, Jesus, as payment for our sins, 1 John 4:10)

List some of the attributes of God's love *(agape)* that you find in 1 Corinthians 13.
(See 1 Corinthians 13 for a list)

Review the "Day 10 Diagram" and ask if there are any questions. Ask each family member to share his or her diagram.
(A completed Diagram is on the next page for your reference.)

Ask if anyone has a personal prayer need that the rest of the family can pray for this week.

Bible Memory Recommendation (for upcoming week):
1 John 5:13, Psalm 119:160

Close:
Read 1 John 5:13 and Psalm 119:160.
Close in prayer as a family by going around the circle first, in Adoration, then Confession, then Thanksgiving, and concluding with Supplication.

Title: **God is Love**
Key Verse: 1 John 4:10

Chapter: **Four**
♥: 1 John 4:7-19, Phil 3:8-11
2 Cor. 5:14-15, Eph 5:1-4

Greek Words: Love
Agape: God's Love, Unconditional
Storgay: Parent
Eros: Marriage
Phileo: Friend

• Darkness
• Antichrist
• False Prophets
• Haters of Brothers
• Liars

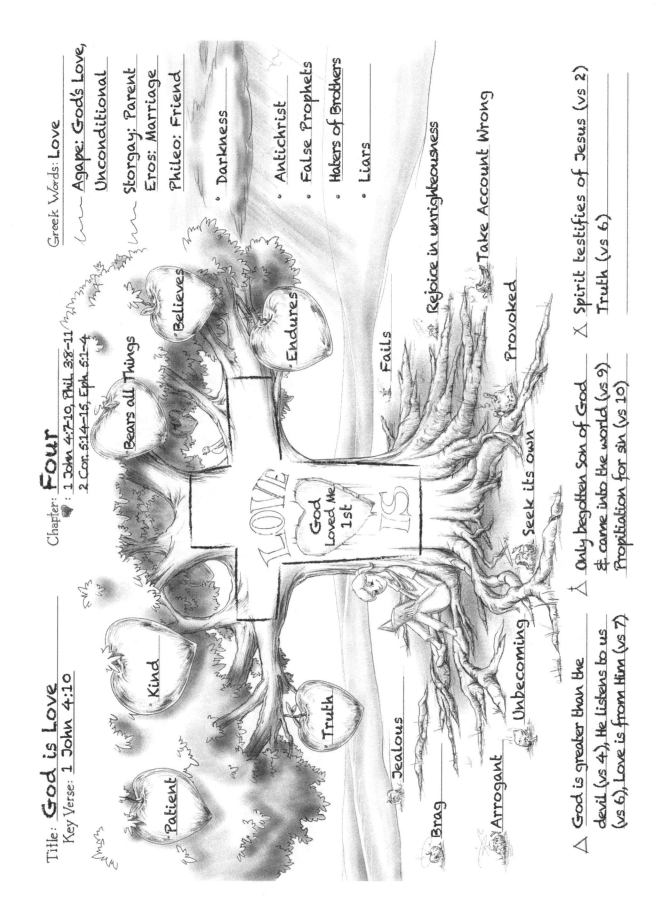

Believes
Endures
Bears all Things
Patient
Kind
Truth

LOVE IS
God Loved Me 1st

Jealous
Brag
Arrogant
Unbecoming
Seek its own
Provoked
Take Account Wrong
Rejoice in unrighteousness
Fails

△ God is greater than the devil (vs 4), He listens to us (vs 6), Love is from Him (vs 7)

† Only begotten Son of God & came into the world (vs 9) Propitiation for sin (vs 10)

✗ Spirit testifies of Jesus (vs 2) Truth (vs 6)

W E E K   T E N

"GET READY!"

Prepare: Complete Senior Sword Study Week 10 **OR** read 1 John - read Chapter 5 twice.

Write: 1 John 5:1-13 is the writing task for this week.

Quick Notes: Everyone rounded the corner and headed for home this week as they dug into the final chapter of 1 John. Day 1 began with interviewing the chapter using the 5 W's and H. From their questioning, they found that John presented three witnesses of Jesus' deity: the Spirit, water and blood. The students spent three days looking at baptism and the power of Christ's death. Finally, they concluded the week looking at the attributes of liars and truth since John has mentioned both throughout the book of 1 John. We chose 1 John 5:13 as the key verse.

Summary: During the Levitical times, a person had to present two to three witnesses to prove a case against another. John moves from a call to love God, to our ability as His children to overcome the world through our belief in Jesus. Once again, John circles back to a previous point. His initial verses proclaimed his personal witness of Jesus. In Chapter 5, he proclaims even better witnesses for his defense of Jesus' presence on earth as God's Son. Even better, they witness that those who believe in Jesus as the Word of Life, will receive eternal life. Jesus is God and in Him there is eternal life - this is truth. Thus, he closes his debate with the Gnostic, false prophets. John has made his case, a true repetition of the Gospel, which was a message from Jesus Himself. Jesus is the way, the truth and the life. No man will come to the Father except through Jesus.

Creative Family Ideas for the weekend – Theme: "Washing & Cleaning"

• Pull out some tarnished silverware and polish it.

• Note the differences in your pennies from last week.

• Do tie-dyed shirts, talk about how the white under the rubberbands stays clean.

• Go on a street evangelizing trip as a family.

• Watch Ray Comfort's "Roots" series.

• Discuss baptism. Give an opportunity for any members who haven't been baptized to do so.

W E E K   T E N

Begin with Prayer

Read Scripture:
Read John 14 and Psalm 51:5-7

Worship:
Sing hymns and/or worship songs
Share memorized verses

Family Discussion Questions:

Who overcomes the world?
(Those that believe in Jesus overcome the world, 1 John 5:5)

What are the three witnesses?
(The Spirit, the water and the blood, 1 John 5:8)

What does baptism symbolize? What does it declare?
(Baptism symbolizes the washing away of sins and the commitment, with the Spirit's help, to die to self and one's past. Baptism is also a public declaration of new life and a relationship with God through belief in Jesus Christ.)

What is prayer?
(Talking to God.)

How do we know that God hears our prayers?
(We know that if we ask according to His will, He hears us, 1 John 5:14)

What is the final warning of 1 John?
(We are to guard ourselves from idols, 1 John 5:21)

Ask if anyone has a personal prayer need that the rest of the family can pray for this week.

Bible Memory Recommendation (for upcoming week):
Romans 4:7-8, Matthew 22:36-40

Close:
Read Romans 4:7-8 and Matthew 22:36-40.
Close in prayer as a family by going around the circle, first in Adoration, then Confession, then Thanksgiving, and concluding with Supplication.

WEEK ELEVEN

"GET READY!"

Prepare: Complete Senior Sword Study Week 11 **OR** read 1 John and mark any references to God in Chapter 5.

Write: Finish copying the final verses of 1 John 5.

Quick Notes: All levels wrapped up their Sword Study of 1 John with word studies of **believe** and **understanding**. These two words in the Greek were not chosen for their repetitive nature, but for their importance to John's letter. They were a part of his summary statements to his readers: "Believe in Jesus, He will give you understanding." After learning the definitions, the students cemented their understanding of the Greek words through cross reference exercises.

Summary: As we come to the conclusion of 1 John, we hear our fatherly teacher summarize his message, once again. "Children of God, you know God because you believe in His Son, Jesus. Jesus will give you knowledge and understanding. You have eternal life through your faith in His work on the cross." The truth of his message resounds through the pages of 1 John to us just as it did to the readers of his day. As children of God, we have an intimate relationship with Jesus that gives us fellowship with the Father, love for others and a walk that abides with and models our Savior.

Creative Family Ideas for the weekend – Theme: "Believe... Have Faith!"

• Find and paint rocks with the word "Believe" or "Faith." Then, decorate your garden or flower beds with them as a reminder of your relationship with God through Jesus.

• Play games that require trust, such as Follow-the-Leader with a twist - blindfold all the members of your family, except the leader!

• Purchase a Scritpure wall stencil to place in prominent location in your home to proclaim your families faith in Christ.

• Make an acrostic for the word "believe."

W E E K   E L E V E N

Begin with Prayer

Read Scripture:
    Read Psalm 36:5-10 and Romans 4:7-8

Worship:
    Sing hymns and/or worship songs
    Share memorized verses

Family Discussion Questions:

    What must we believe to be a child of God?
    (We must believe that Jesus is the Christ, 1 John 5:1)

    What does the word believe mean?
    (To have faith in or entrust one's spiritual well-being in Christ)

    What does the word faith mean?
    (Conviction or belief ... Christians have reliance on Christ for salvation)

    If we believe in Jesus, what can we know that we have from God, the Father?
    (Eternal life, 1 John 5:13)

    Review the "Day 10 Diagram" and ask if there are any questions. Ask each family member to share his or her diagram.
    (A completed Diagram is on the next page for your reference.)

    Ask if anyone has a personal prayer need that the rest of the family can pray for this week.

Bible Memory Recommendation (for upcoming week):
    Matthew 5:14-16, Hosea 6:3-6

Close:
    Read Matthew 5:14-16 and Hosea 6:3-6.
    Close in prayer as a family by going around the circle, first in Adoration, then Confession, then Thanksgiving, and concluding with Supplication.

Title: I Have Eternal Life!
Key Verse: 1 John 5:13

Chapter: Five
♥: 1 John 5:13, Ps. 119:160
Romans 4:7-8, Matt 22:35-40

Greek Words: Believe &
 Understanding
Pisteuo(V): Believe,
Entrust
Pistis(N): Faith
Dianoia: Mature,
Deep Thought

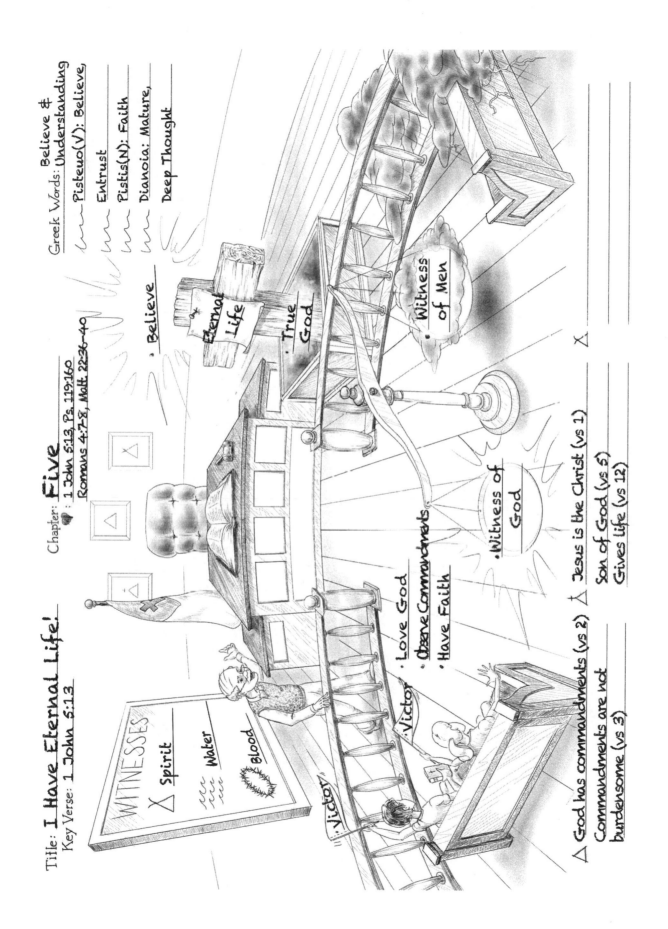

• Believe

Eternal
Life

• True
God

Witness
of Men

Witness
of God

• Love God
• Observe Commandments
• Have Faith

• Victory

•: Victory

WITNESSES
X Spirit
∼∼ Water
Blood

△ God has commandments (vs 2)   ⋏ Jesus is the Christ (vs 1)
Commandments are not   Son of God (vs 5)
burdensome (vs 3)   Gives Life (vs 12)
                                           X

W E E K   T W E L V E

"GET READY!"

Prepare: Complete Senior Sword Study Week 12 **OR** read 1 John.

Quick Notes: Having completed the in-depth study of 1 John, students have spent the week refreshing their memories of each chapter's details by completing blank copies of the five Day 10 Diagrams. They have looked back at their prayer notes to see all that the Lord has taught them through their study of 1 John.

Creative Family Ideas for the weekend – Theme: "Washing & Cleaning"

• Watch the DVD, "St. John in Exile," with Dean Jones.

• Plan to have a mock Bible Bee using your 1 John Bible Memory Cards at your upcoming weekend Family Bonfire. All you need is a table with two chairs for the "official Judges," and chairs for the audience at the back of your room. Each child can take turns saying a memory passage.

• You could invite family and friends over for some fellowship and Bible Memory presentations!

• Consider participating in the National Bible Bee with your family next summer. The event is sponsored by The Shelby Kennedy Foundation, and encourages and equips families to deepen their relationships with Christ through God's Word. Plus, it's a lot of fun with fellow followers of Jesus!

WEEK TWELVE

Begin with Prayer

Read Scripture:
Read Psalm 111 and Jeremiah 9:23-24

Worship:
Sing hymns and/or worship songs
Share memorized verses

Family Discussion Questions:

What do you remember about John? *(Fisherman, Son of Zebedee, Brother to James, Matthew 4:17-24; Disciple of Jesus Christ, Matthew 10:1-2; Present with Jesus during transfiguration, Mark 9:1-2; Part of Jesus' inner circle, close friend, Mark 14:31-41; Prisoner on Patmos and Bondservant of God, Revelation 1:1, 9-11)*

John made two comparisons in 1 John 1; he compared light with _____ and truth with _____? *(Light to darkness, 1 John 1:5 and Truth to lie, 1 John 1:6)*

What is sin? *(An action against God's rules)*

Who has sinned? *(Everyone has sinned, Romans 3:23)*

What are some of the titles that John used for his recipients? *(Little children, Fathers, Young men, Beloved)*

Why do we need propitiation from God? *(Our sins, 1 John 2:2)*

What does the word *abide* mean? *(To dwell, live, remain with another in mind, heart and will)*

Because God loves us so much, what does He call us? *(His children, 1 John 3:1)*

What is the definition of righteous? *(Doing what is right according to God's rules)*

Who loved first? Did God love us, or did we love God? *(God loved us first, 1 John 4:19)*

What is *agape* love? *(God-like love that is of the will, self-sacrificing, compassionate and unconditional)*

What did God's love do for us? *(Sent His Son, Jesus, as payment for our sins, 1 John 4:10)*

Ask if anyone has a personal prayer need that the rest of the family can pray for this week.

Bible Memory Recommendation:
Review your Bible Memory Passages in some unique way.

Close: Read Psalm 51:1-10
Close in prayer as a family by going around the circle first, in Adoration, then Confession, then Thanksgiving, and concluding with Supplication.

MY COPY OF 1 JOHN

GOD
the Father

GOD
the Son

GOD
the Holy Spirit

GOD
the Father

GOD
the Son

GOD
the Holy Spirit

GOD
the Father

GOD
the Son

GOD
the Holy Spirit

GOD
the Father

GOD
the Son

GOD
the Holy Spirit

GOD
the Father

GOD
the Son

GOD
the Holy Spirit

GOD
the Father

GOD
the Son

GOD
the Holy Spirit

GOD
the Father

GOD
the Son

GOD
the Holy Spirit

GOD
the Father

GOD
the Son

GOD
the Holy Spirit

MEMORY PASSAGES

FOCUS SCRIPTURES

Jeremiah 9:23-24
1 John 5:13

WEEK ONE	WEEK TWO
Psalm 111:10	John 8:12
Jeremiah 9:23-24	John 17:3

WEEK THREE	WEEK FOUR
1 John 1:3	Job 15:14-16
1 John 1:9	Proverbs 28:13-14

WEEK FIVE	WEEK SIX
Psalm 36:7-10	2 Corinthians 6:16-18
John 8:31-32	Isaiah 43:1-2

WEEK SEVEN	WEEK EIGHT
2 Corinthians 5:20-21	1 John 4:7-10
Isaiah 45:22-23	Philippians 3:8-11

WEEK NINE	WEEK TEN
2 Corinthians 5:14-15	1 John 5:13
Ephesians 5:1-4	Psalm 119:160

WEEK ELEVEN	WEEK TWELVE
Romans 4:7-8	Matthew 5:14-16
Matthew 22:36-40	Hosea 6:3-6

An asterisk denotes these passages in the Primary, Junior, and Senior Sword Studies.

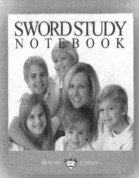

You Can Host
a Summer Bible Bee!

Encourage!
Recognize!
Reward!

FAMILY DISCIPLESHIP
(Cleverly Disguised as a Contest)

Everything you need is provided for three "Encouragement Parties" and the Local Celebration Day in August. Parents receive a Family Guide and each child gets his/her own age-appropriate, 20-minute per day Bible study on June 1st! Support local families as they discover a deeper walk with God through inductive Bible study and hiding His Word in their hearts!

Get details at www.BibleBee.org today!

Did you enjoy this study?

We Still Deliver!

There are three ways to continue your growth...

1. If you have children ages 7-18, join us next Summer for The National Bible Bee.

- All materials delivered to you on June 1st.
- Same inductive study method.
- Same whole-family synchronized materials.
- New Bible book to study each summer.
- Meet like-minded families near you.
- Win great prizes, with over $260,000 awarded at Nationals.

Answer all your questions at www.BibleBee.org

**2. If you just want the next study as soon as it is available,
order it directly from The Shelby Kennedy Foundation at Store.BibleBee.org**

3. Buy one of our other Sword Study titles at your local Christian bookstore.

www.SwordStudy.org | (937) 382-7250
www.BibleBee.org

Psalm 111:10

10 The fear of the LORD is the beginning of wisdom; all those who practice it have a good understanding. His praise endures forever!

Psalm 111:10

Week 1   ESV

John 8:12

12 Again Jesus spoke to them, saying, "I am the light of the world. Whoever follows me will not walk in darkness, but will have the light of life."

John 8:12

Week 2   ESV

1 John 1:3

3 that which we have seen and heard we proclaim also to you, so that you too may have fellowship with us; and indeed our fellowship is with the Father and with his Son Jesus Christ.

1 John 1:3

Week 3   ESV

Job 15:14-16

14 What is man, that he can be pure? Or he who is born of a woman, that he can be righteous? 15 Behold, God puts no trust in his holy ones, and the heavens are not pure in his sight; 16 how much less one who is abominable and corrupt, a man who drinks injustice like water!

Job 15:14-16

Week 4   ESV

Psalm 36:7-10

7 How precious is your steadfast love, O God! The children of mankind take refuge in the shadow of your wings. 8 They feast on the abundance of your house, and you give them drink from the river of your delights. 9 For with you is the fountain of life; in your light do we see light. 10 Oh, continue your steadfast love to those who know you, and your righteousness to the upright of heart!

Psalm 36:7-10

Week 5   ESV

Isaiah 43:1-2

1 But now thus says the LORD, he who created you, O Jacob, he who formed you, O Israel: "Fear not, for I have redeemed you; I have called you by name, you are mine. 2 When you pass through the waters, I will be with you; and through the rivers, they shall not overwhelm you; when you walk through fire you shall not be burned, and the flame shall not consume you.

Isaiah 43:1-2

Week 6   ESV

John 17:3

3 And this is eternal life, that they know you the only true God, and Jesus Christ whom you have sent.

John 17:3

Week 2   ESV

Jeremiah 9:23-24

23 Thus says the LORD: "Let not the wise man boast in his wisdom, let not the mighty man boast in his might, let not the rich man boast in his riches, 24 but let him who boasts boast in this, that he understands and knows me, that I am the LORD who practices steadfast love, justice, and righteousness in the earth. For in these things I delight, declares the LORD."

Jeremiah 9:23-24

Week 1   ESV

Proverbs 28:13-14

13 Whoever conceals his transgressions will not prosper, but he who confesses and forsakes them will obtain mercy. 14 Blessed is the one who fears the LORD always, but whoever hardens his heart will fall into calamity.

Proverbs 28:13-14

Week 4   ESV

1 John 1:9

9 If we confess our sins, he is faithful and just to forgive us our sins and to cleanse us from all unrighteousness.

1 John 1:9

Week 3   ESV

2 Corinthians 6:16-18

16 What agreement has the temple of God with idols? For we are the temple of the living God; as God said, "I will make my dwelling among them and walk among them, and I will be their God, and they shall be my people. 17 Therefore go out from their midst, and be separate from them, says the Lord, and touch no unclean thing; then I will welcome you, 18 and I will be a father to you, and you shall be sons and daughters to me, says the Lord Almighty."

2 Corinthians 6:16-18

Week 6   ESV

John 8:31-32

31 So Jesus said to the Jews who had believed him, "If you abide in my word, you are truly my disciples, 32 and you will know the truth, and the truth will set you free."

John 8:31-32

Week 5   ESV

ESV

Isaiah 45:22-23

22 "Turn to me and be saved, all the ends of the earth! For I am God, and there is no other. 23 By myself I have sworn; from my mouth has gone out in righteousness a word that shall not return: 'To me every knee shall bow, every tongue shall swear allegiance.'

Isaiah 45:22-23

Week 7   ESV

Philippians 3:8-11

8 Indeed, I count everything as loss because of the surpassing worth of knowing Christ Jesus my Lord. For his sake I have suffered the loss of all things and count them as rubbish, in order that I may gain Christ 9 and be found in him, not having a righteousness of my own that comes from the law, but that which comes through faith in Christ, the righteousness from God that depends on faith— 10 that I may know him and the power of his resurrection, and may share his sufferings, becoming like him in his death, 11 that by any means possible I may attain the resurrection from the dead.

Philippians 3:8-11

Week 8   ESV

2 Corinthians 5:14-15

14 For the love of Christ controls us, because we have concluded this: that one has died for all, therefore all have died; 15 and he died for all, that those who live might no longer live for themselves but for him who for their sake died and was raised.

2 Corinthians 5:14-15

Week 9   ESV

Psalm 119:160

160 The sum of your word is truth, and every one of your righteous rules endures forever.

Psalm 119:160

Week 10   ESV

Matthew 22:36-40

36 "Teacher, which is the great commandment in the Law?" 37 And he said to him, "You shall love the Lord your God with all your heart and with all your soul and with all your mind. 38 This is the great and first commandment. 39 And a second is like it: You shall love your neighbor as yourself. 40 On these two commandments depend all the Law and the Prophets."

Matthew 22:36-40

Week 11   ESV

Hosea 6:3-6

3 Let us know; let us press on to know the LORD; his going out is sure as the dawn; he will come to us as the showers, as the spring rains that water the earth." 4 What shall I do with you, O Ephraim? What shall I do with you, O Judah? Your love is like a morning cloud, like the dew that goes early away. 5 Therefore I have hewn them by the prophets; I have slain them by the words of my mouth, and my judgment goes forth as the light. 6 For I desire steadfast love and not sacrifice, the knowledge of God rather than burnt offerings.

Hosea 6:3-6

Week 12   ESV

The SHELBY KENNEDY Foundation

ESV

1 John 4:7-10

7 Beloved, let us love one another, for love is from God, and whoever loves has been born of God and knows God. 8 Anyone who does not love does not know God, because God is love. 9 In this the love of God was made manifest among us, that God sent his only Son into the world, so that we might live through him. 10 In this is love, not that we have loved God but that he loved us and sent his Son to be the propitiation for our sins.

1 John 4:7-10

Week 8   ESV

2 Corinthians 5:20-21

20 Therefore, we are ambassadors for Christ, God making his appeal through us. We implore you on behalf of Christ, be reconciled to God. 21 For our sake he made him to be sin who knew no sin, so that in him we might become the righteousness of God.

2 Corinthians 5:20-21

Week 7   ESV

1 John 5:13

13 I write these things to you who believe in the name of the Son of God that you may know that you have eternal life.

1 John 5:13

Week 10   ESV

Ephesians 5:1-4

1 Therefore be imitators of God, as beloved children. 2 And walk in love, as Christ loved us and gave himself up for us, a fragrant offering and sacrifice to God. 3 But sexual immorality and all impurity or covetousness must not even be named among you, as is proper among saints. 4 Let there be no filthiness nor foolish talk nor crude joking, which are out of place, but instead let there be thanksgiving.

Ephesians 5:1-4

Week 9   ESV

Matthew 5:14-16

14 "You are the light of the world. A city set on a hill cannot be hidden. 15 Nor do people light a lamp and put it under a basket, but on a stand, and it gives light to all in the house. 16 In the same way, let your light shine before others, so that they may see your good works and give glory to your Father who is in heaven.

Matthew 5:14-16

Week 12   ESV

Acts 10:38-43

38 how God anointed Jesus of Nazareth with the Holy Spirit and with power. He went about doing good and healing all who were oppressed by the devil, for God was with him. 39 And we are witnesses of all that he did both in the country of the Jews and in Jerusalem. They put him to death by hanging him on a tree, 40 but God raised him on the third day and made him to appear, 41 not to all the people but to us who had been chosen by God as witnesses, who ate and drank with him after he rose from the dead. 42 And he commanded us to preach to the people and to testify that he is the one appointed by God to be judge of the living and the dead. 43 To him all the prophets bear witness that everyone who believes in him receives forgiveness of sins through his name."

Acts 10:38-43

Week 11   ESV

Psalm 111:10

10 The fear of the LORD is the beginning of wisdom: a good understanding have all they that do his commandments: his praise endureth for ever.

Psalm 111:10

Week 1   KJV

John 8:12

12 Then spake Jesus again unto them, saying, I am the light of the world: he that followeth me shall not walk in darkness, but shall have the light of life.

John 8:12

Week 2   KJV

1 John 1:3

3 That which we have seen and heard declare we unto you, that ye also may have fellowship with us: and truly our fellowship is with the Father, and with his Son Jesus Christ.

1 John 1:3

Week 3   KJV

Job 15:14-16

14 What is man, that he should be clean? and he which is born of a woman, that he should be righteous? 15 Behold, he putteth no trust in his saints; yea, the heavens are not clean in his sight. 16 How much more abominable and filthy is man, which drinketh iniquity like water?

Job 15:14-16

Week 4   KJV

Psalm 36:7-10

7 How excellent is thy lovingkindness, O God! therefore the children of men put their trust under the shadow of thy wings. 8 They shall be abundantly satisfied with the fatness of thy house; and thou shalt make them drink of the river of thy pleasures. 9 For with thee is the fountain of life: in thy light shall we see light. 10 O continue thy lovingkindness unto them that know thee; and thy righteousness to the upright in heart.

Psalm 36:7-10

Week 5   KJV

Isaiah 43:1-2

1 But now thus saith the LORD that created thee, O Jacob, and he that formed thee, O Israel, Fear not: for I have redeemed thee, I have called thee by thy name; thou art mine. 2 When thou passest through the waters, I will be with thee; and through the rivers, they shall not overflow thee: when thou walkest through the fire, thou shalt not be burned; neither shall the flame kindle upon thee.

Isaiah 43:1-2

Week 6   KJV

John 17:3

3 And this is life eternal, that they might know thee the only true God, and Jesus Christ, whom thou hast sent.

John 17:3

Week 2   KJV

Jeremiah 9:23-24

23 Thus saith the LORD, Let not the wise man glory in his wisdom, neither let the mighty man glory in his might, let not the rich man glory in his riches: 24 But let him that glorieth glory in this, that he understandeth and knoweth me, that I am the LORD which exercise lovingkindness, judgment, and righteousness, in the earth: for in these things I delight, saith the LORD.

Jeremiah 9:23-24

Week 1   KJV

Proverbs 28:13-14

13 He that covereth his sins shall not prosper: but whoso confesseth and forsaketh them shall have mercy. 14 Happy is the man that feareth always: but he that hardeneth his heart shall fall into mischief.

Proverbs 28:13-14

Week 4   KJV

1 John 1:9

9 If we confess our sins, he is faithful and just to forgive us our sins, and to cleanse us from all unrighteousness.

1 John 1:9

Week 3   KJV

2 Corinthians 6:16-18

16 And what agreement hath the temple of God with idols? for ye are the temple of the living God; as God hath said, I will dwell in them, and walk in them; and I will be their God, and they shall be my people. 17 Wherefore come out from among them, and be ye separate, saith the Lord, and touch not the unclean thing; and I will receive you, 18 And will be a Father unto you, and ye shall be my sons and daughters, saith the Lord Almighty.

2 Corinthians 6:16-18

Week 6   KJV

John 8:31-32

31 Then said Jesus to those Jews which believed on him, If ye continue in my word, then are ye my disciples indeed; 32 And ye shall know the truth, and the truth shall make you free.

John 8:31-32

Week 5   KJV

Isaiah 45:22-23

22 Look unto me, and be ye saved, all the ends of the earth: for I am God, and there is none else. 23 I have sworn by myself, the word is gone out of my mouth in righteousness, and shall not return, That unto me every knee shall bow, every tongue shall swear.

Isaiah 45:22-23

Week 7 KJV

Philippians 3:8-11

8 Yea doubtless, and I count all things but loss for the excellency of the knowledge of Christ Jesus my Lord: for whom I have suffered the loss of all things, and do count them but dung, that I may win Christ, 9 And be found in him, not having mine own righteousness, which is of the law, but that which is through the faith of Christ, the righteousness which is of God by faith: 10 That I may know him, and the power of his resurrection, and the fellowship of his sufferings, being made conformable unto his death; 11 If by any means I might attain unto the resurrection of the dead.

Philippians 3:8-11

Week 8   KJV

2 Corinthians 5:14-15

14 For the love of Christ constraineth us; because we thus judge, that if one died for all, then were all dead: 15 And that he died for all, that they which live should not henceforth live unto themselves, but unto him which died for them, and rose again.

2 Corinthians 5:14-15

Week 9 KJV

Psalm 119:160

160 Thy word is true from the beginning: and every one of thy righteous judgments endureth for ever.

Psalm 119:160

Wcck 10   KJV

Matthew 22:36-40

36 Master, which is the great commandment in the law? 37 Jesus said unto him, Thou shalt love the Lord thy God with all thy heart, and with all thy soul, and with all thy mind. 38 This is the first and great commandment. 39 And the second is like unto it, Thou shalt love thy neighbour as thyself. 40 On these two commandments hang all the law and the prophets.

Matthew 22:36-40

Week 11 KJV

Hosea 6:3-6

3 Then shall we know, if we follow on to know the LORD: his going forth is prepared as the morning; and he shall come unto us as the rain, as the latter and former rain unto the earth. 4 O Ephraim, what shall I do unto thee? O Judah, what shall I do unto thee? for your goodness is as a morning cloud, and as the early dew it goeth away. 5 Therefore have I hewed them by the prophets; I have slain them by the words of my mouth: and thy judgments are as the light that goeth forth. 6 For I desired mercy, and not sacrifice; and the knowledge of God more than burnt offerings.

Hosea 6:3-6

Week 12   KJV

1 John 4:7-10

7 Beloved, let us love one another: for love is of God; and every one that loveth is born of God, and knoweth God. 8 He that loveth not knoweth not God; for God is love. 9 In this was manifested the Love of God toward us, because that God sent his only begotten Son into the world, that we might live through him. 10 Herein is Love, not that we loved God, but that he loved us, and sent his Son To be the propitiation for our sins.

1 John 4:7-10

Week 8 KJV

2 Corinthians 5:20-21

20 Now then we are ambassadors for Christ, as though God did beseech you by us: we pray you in Christ's stead, be ye reconciled to God. 21 For he hath made him to be sin for us, who knew no sin; that we might be made the righteousness of God in him.

2 Corinthians 5:20-21

Week 7 KJV

1 John 5:13

13 These things have I written unto you that believe on the name of the Son of God; that ye may know that ye have eternal life, and that ye may believe on the name of the Son of God.

1 John 5:13

Week 10 KJV

Ephesians 5:1-4

1 Be ye therefore followers of God, as dear children; 2 And walk in love, as Christ also hath loved us, and hath given himself for us an offering and a sacrifice to God for a sweetsmelling savour. 3 But fornication, and all uncleanness, or covetousness, let it not be once named among you, as becometh saints; 4 Neither filthiness, nor foolish talking, nor jesting, which are not convenient: but rather giving of thanks.

Ephesians 5:1-4

Week 9 KJV

Matthew 5:14-16

14 Ye are the light of the world. A city that is set on an hill cannot be hid. 15 Neither do men light a candle, and put it under a bushel, but on a candlestick; and it giveth light unto all that are in the house. 16 Let your light so shine before men, that they may see your good works, and glorify your Father which is in heaven.

Matthew 5:14-16

Week 12 KJV

Acts 10:38-43

38 How God anointed Jesus of Nazareth with the Holy Ghost and with power: who went about doing good, and healing all that were oppressed of the devil; for God was with him. 39 And we are witnesses of all things which he did both in the land of the Jews, and in Jerusalem; whom they slew and hanged on a tree: 40 Him God raised up the third day, and showed him openly; 41 Not to all the people, but unto witnesses chosen before of God, even to us, who did eat and drink with him after he rose from the dead. 42 And he commanded us to preach unto the people, and to testify that it is he which was ordained of God to be the Judge of quick and dead. 43 To him give all the prophets witness, that through his name whosoever believeth in him shall receive remission of sins.

Acts 10:38-43

Week 11 KJV

Psalm 111:10

10 The fear of the LORD is the beginning of wisdom;
A good understanding have all those who do His
commandments; His praise endures forever.

Psalm 111:10

Week 1   NASB

John 8:12

12 Then Jesus again spoke to them, saying, " I am the
Light of the world; he who follows Me will not walk in the
darkness, but will have the Light of life."

John 8:12

Week 2   NASB

1 John 1:3

3 what we have seen and heard we proclaim to you also, so
that you too may have fellowship with us; and indeed our
fellowship is with the Father, and with His Son Jesus Christ.

1 John 1:3

Week 3   NASB

Job 15:14-16

14 "What is man, that he should be pure, Or he who is born
of a woman, that he should be righteous? 15 "Behold, He
puts no trust in His holy ones, And the heavens are not pure
in His sight; 16 How much less one who is detestable and
corrupt, Man, who drinks iniquity like water!

Job 15:14-16

Week 4   NASB

Psalm 36:7-10

7 How precious is Your lovingkindness, O God! And the
children of men take refuge in the shadow of Your wings. 8
They drink their fill of the abundance of Your house; And
You give them to drink of the river of Your delights. 9 For
with You is the fountain of life; In Your light we see light. 10
O continue Your lovingkindness to those who know You,
And Your righteousness to the upright in heart.

Psalm 36:7-10

Week 5   NASB

Isaiah 43:1-2

1 But now, thus says the LORD, your Creator, O Jacob,
And He who formed you, O Israel, "Do not fear, for I have
redeemed you; I have called you by name; you are Mine! 2
"When you pass through the waters, I will be with you; And
through the rivers, they will not overflow you. When you
walk through the fire, you will not be scorched, Nor will the
flame burn you.

Isaiah 43:1-2

Week 6   NASB

John 17:3

3 "This is eternal life, that they may know You, the only true God, and Jesus Christ whom You have sent.

John 17:3

Week 2   NASB

Jeremiah 9:23-24

3 Thus says the LORD, " Let not a wise man boast of his wisdom, and let not the mighty man boast of his might, let not a rich man boast of his riches; 24 but let him who boasts boast of this, that he understands and knows Me, that I am the LORD who exercises lovingkindness, justice and righteousness on earth; for I delight in these things," declares the LORD.

Jeremiah 9:23-24

Week 1   NASB

Proverbs 28:13-14

3 He who conceals his transgressions will not prosper, But he who confesses and forsakes them will find compassion. 14 How blessed is the man who fears always, But he who hardens his heart will fall into calamity.

Proverbs 28:13-14

Week 4   NASB

1 John 1:9

9 If we confess our sins, He is faithful and righteous to forgive us our sins and to cleanse us from all unrighteousness.

1 John 1:9

Week 3   NASB

2 Corinthians 6:16-18

16 Or what agreement has the temple of God with idols? For we are the temple of the living God; just as God said, " I WILL DWELL IN THEM AND WALK AMONG THEM; AND I WILL BE THEIR GOD, AND THEY SHALL BE MY PEOPLE. 17 " Therefore, COME OUT FROM THEIR MIDST AND BE SEPARATE," says the Lord. "AND DO NOT TOUCH WHAT IS UNCLEAN; And I will welcome you. 18 " And I will be a father to you, And you shall be sons and daughters to Me," Says the Lord Almighty.

2 Corinthians 6:16-18

Week 6   NASB

John 8:31-32

31 So Jesus was saying to those Jews who had believed Him, " If you continue in My word, then you are truly disciples of Mine; 32 and you will know the truth, and the truth will make you free."

John 8:31-32

Week 5   NASB

The SHELBY KENNEDY Foundation

Isaiah 45:22-23

22 " Turn to Me and be saved, all the ends of the earth; For I am God, and there is no other. 23 " I have sworn by Myself, The word has gone forth from My mouth in righteousness And will not turn back, That to Me every knee will bow, every tongue will swear allegiance.

Isaiah 45:22-23

Week 7   NASB

Philippians 3:8-11

8 More than that, I count all things to be loss in view of the surpassing value of knowing Christ Jesus my Lord, for whom I have suffered the loss of all things, and count them but rubbish so that I may gain Christ, 9 and may be found in Him, not having a righteousness of my own derived from the Law, but that which is through faith in Christ, the righteousness which comes from God on the basis of faith, 10 that I may know Him and the power of His resurrection and the fellowship of His sufferings, being conformed to His death; 11 in order that I may attain to the resurrection from the dead.

Philippians 3:8-11

Week 8   NASB

2 Corinthians 5:14-15

14 For the love of Christ controls us, having concluded this, that one died for all, therefore all died; 15 and He died for all, so that they who live might no longer live for themselves, but for Him who died and rose again on their behalf.

2 Corinthians 5:14-15

Week 9   NASB

Psalm 119:160

160 The sum of Your word is truth, And every one of Your righteous ordinances is everlasting.

Psalm 119:160

Week 10   NASB

Matthew 22:36-40

36 "Teacher, which is the great commandment in the Law?" 37 And He said to him, " ' YOU SHALL LOVE THE LORD YOUR GOD WITH ALL YOUR HEART, AND WITH ALL YOUR SOUL, AND WITH ALL YOUR MIND.' 38 "This is the great and foremost commandment. 39 "The second is like it, 'YOU SHALL LOVE YOUR NEIGHBOR AS YOURSELF.' 40 "On these two commandments depend the whole Law and the Prophets."

Matthew 22:36-40

Week 11   NASB

Hosea 6:3-6

3 "So let us know, let us press on to know the LORD. His going forth is as certain as the dawn; And He will come to us like the rain, Like the spring rain watering the earth." 4 What shall I do with you, O Ephraim? What shall I do with you, O Judah? For your loyalty is like a morning cloud And like the dew which goes away early. 5 Therefore I have hewn them in pieces by the prophets; I have slain them by the words of My mouth; And the judgments on you are like the light that goes forth. 6 For I delight in loyalty rather than sacrifice, And in the knowledge of God rather than burnt offerings.

Hosea 6:3-6

Week 12   NASB

1 John 4:7-10

7 Beloved, let us love one another, for love is from God; and everyone who loves is born of God and knows God. 8 The one who does not love does not know God, for God is love. 9 By this the love of God was manifested in us, that God has sent His only begotten Son into the world so that we might live through Him. 10 In this is love, not that we loved God, but that He loved us and sent His Son to be the propitiation for our sins.

1 John 4:7-10

Week 8 NASB

2 Corinthians 5:20-21

20 Therefore, we are ambassadors for Christ, as though God were making an appeal through us; we beg you on behalf of Christ, be reconciled to God. 21 He made Him who knew no sin to be sin on our behalf, so that we might become the righteousness of God in Him.

2 Corinthians 5:20-21

Week 7 NASB

1 John 5:13

13 These things I have written to you who believe in the name of the Son of God, so that you may know that you have eternal life.

1 John 5:13

Week 10 NASB

Ephesians 5:1-4

1 Therefore be imitators of God, as beloved children; 2 and walk in love, just as Christ also loved you and gave Himself up for us, an offering and a sacrifice to God as a fragrant aroma. 3 But immorality or any impurity or greed must not even be named among you, as is proper among saints; 4 and there must be no filthiness and silly talk, or coarse jesting, which are not fitting, but rather giving of thanks.

Ephesians 5:1-4

Week 9 NASB

Matthew 5:14-16

14 "You are the light of the world. A city set on a hill cannot be hidden; 15 nor does anyone light a lamp and put it under a basket, but on the lampstand, and it gives light to all who are in the house. 16 "Let your light shine before men in such a way that they may see your good works, and glorify your Father who is in heaven.

Matthew 5:14-16

Week 12 NASB

Acts 10:38-43

38 "You know of Jesus of Nazareth, how God anointed Him with the Holy Spirit and with power, and how He went about doing good and healing all who were oppressed by the devil, for God was with Him. 39 "We are witnesses of all the things He did both in the land of the Jews and in Jerusalem. They also put Him to death by hanging Him on a cross. 40 "God raised Him up on the third day and granted that He become visible, 41 not to all the people, but to witnesses who were chosen beforehand by God, that is, to us who ate and drank with Him after He arose from the dead. 42 "And He ordered us to preach to the people, and solemnly to testify that this is the One who has been appointed by God as Judge of the living and the dead. 43 Of Him all the prophets bear witness that through His name everyone who believes in Him receives forgiveness of sins."

Acts 10:38-43

Week 11 NASB

The SHELBY KENNEDY Foundation

NKJV

Psalm 111:10

10 The fear of the LORD is the beginning of wisdom; A good understanding have all those who do His commandments. His praise endures forever.

Psalm 111:10

Week 1 NKJV

John 8:12

12 Then Jesus spoke to them again, saying, "I am the light of the world. He who follows Me shall not walk in darkness, but have the light of life."

John 8:12

Week 2 NKJV

1 John 1:3

3 that which we have seen and heard we declare to you, that you also may have fellowship with us; and truly our fellowship is with the Father and with His Son Jesus Christ.

1 John 1:3

Week 3 NKJV

Job 15:14-16

14 "What is man, that he could be pure? And he who is born of a woman, that he could be righteous? 15 If God puts no trust in His saints, And the heavens are not pure in His sight, 16 How much less man, who is abominable and filthy, Who drinks iniquity like water!

Job 15:14-16

Week 4 NKJV

Psalm 36:7-10

7 How precious is Your lovingkindness, O God! Therefore the children of men put their trust under the shadow of Your wings. 8 They are abundantly satisfied with the fullness of Your house, And You give them drink from the river of Your pleasures. 9 For with You is the fountain of life; In Your light we see light. 10 Oh, continue Your lovingkindness to those who know You, And Your righteousness to the upright in heart.

Psalm 36:7-10

Week 5 NKJV

Isaiah 43:1-2

1 But now, thus says the LORD, who created you, O Jacob, And He who formed you, O Israel: "Fear not, for I have redeemed you; I have called you by your name; You are Mine. 2 When you pass through the waters, I will be with you; And through the rivers, they shall not overflow you. When you walk through the fire, you shall not be burned, Nor shall the flame scorch you.

Isaiah 43:1-2

Week 6 NKJV

The Shelby Kennedy Foundation

NKJV

John 17:3

3 And this is eternal life, that they may know You, the only true God, and Jesus Christ whom You have sent.

John 17:3

Week 2   NKJV

Jeremiah 9:23-24

23 Thus says the LORD: "Let not the wise man glory in his wisdom, Let not the mighty man glory in his might, Nor let the rich man glory in his riches; 24 But let him who glories glory in this, That he understands and knows Me, That I am the LORD, exercising lovingkindness, judgment, and righteousness in the earth. For in these I delight," says the LORD.

Jeremiah 9:23-24

Week 1   NKJV

Proverbs 28:13-14

13 He who covers his sins will not prosper, But whoever confesses and forsakes them will have mercy. 14 Happy is the man who is always reverent, But he who hardens his heart will fall into calamity.

Proverbs 28:13-14

Week 4   NKJV

1 John 1:9

9 If we confess our sins, He is faithful and just to forgive us our sins and to cleanse us from all unrighteousness.

1 John 1:9

Week 3   NKJV

2 Corinthians 6:16-18

16 And what agreement has the temple of God with idols? For you are the temple of the living God. As God has said: "I will dwell in them And walk among them. I will be their God, And they shall be My people." 17 Therefore "Come out from among them And be separate, says the Lord. Do not touch what is unclean, And I will receive you." 18 "I will be a Father to you, And you shall be My sons and daughters, Says the LORD Almighty."

2 Corinthians 6:16-18

Week 6   NKJV

John 8:31-32

31 Then Jesus said to those Jews who believed Him, "If you abide in My word, you are My disciples indeed. 32 And you shall know the truth, and the truth shall make you free."

John 8:31-32

Week 5   NKJV

NKJV

Isaiah 45:22-23

22 "Look to Me, and be saved, All you ends of the earth! For I am God, and there is no other. 23 I have sworn by Myself; The word has gone out of My mouth in righteousness, And shall not return, That to Me every knee shall bow, Every tongue shall take an oath.

Isaiah 45:22-23

Week 7 NKJV

Philippians 3:8-11

8 Yet indeed I also count all things loss for the excellence of the knowledge of Christ Jesus my Lord, for whom I have suffered the loss of all things, and count them as rubbish, that I may gain Christ 9 and be found in Him, not having my own righteousness, which is from the law, but that which is through faith in Christ, the righteousness which is from God by faith; 10 that I may know Him and the power of His resurrection, and the fellowship of His sufferings, being conformed to His death, 11 if, by any means, I may attain to the resurrection from the dead.

Philippians 3:8-11

Week 8   NKJV

2 Corinthians 5:14-15

14 For the love of Christ compels us, because we judge thus: that if One died for all, then all died; 15 and He died for all, that those who live should live no longer for themselves, but for Him who died for them and rose again.

2 Corinthians 5:14-15

Week 9 NKJV

Psalm 119:160

160 The entirety of Your word is truth, And every one of Your righteous judgments endures forever.

Psalm 119:160

Wcck 10   NKJV

Matthew 22:36-40

36 "Teacher, which is the great commandment in the law?" 37 Jesus said to him, ""You shall love the LORD your God with all your heart, with all your soul, and with all your mind.' 38 This is the first and great commandment. 39 And the second is like it: "You shall love your neighbor as yourself.' 40 On these two commandments hang all the Law and the Prophets."

Matthew 22:36-40

Week 11 NKJV

Hosea 6:3-6

3 Let us know, Let us pursue the knowledge of the LORD. His going forth is established as the morning; He will come to us like the rain, Like the latter and former rain to the earth. 4 "O Ephraim, what shall I do to you? O Judah, what shall I do to you? For your faithfulness is like a morning cloud, And like the early dew it goes away. 5 Therefore I have hewn them by the prophets, I have slain them by the words of My mouth; And your judgments are like light that goes forth. 6 For I desire mercy and not sacrifice, And the knowledge of God more than burnt offerings.

Hosea 6:3-6

Week 12   NKJV

1 John 4:7-10

7 Beloved, let us love one another, for love is of God; and everyone who loves is born of God and knows God. 8 He who does not love does not know God, for God is love. 9 In this the love of God was manifested toward us, that God has sent His only begotten Son into the world, that we might live through Him. 10 In this is love, not that we loved God, but that He loved us and sent His Son to be the propitiation for our sins.

1 John 4:7-10

Week 8 NKJV

2 Corinthians 5:20-21

20 Now then, we are ambassadors for Christ, as though God were pleading through us: we implore you on Christ's behalf, be reconciled to God. 21 For He made Him who knew no sin to be sin for us, that we might become the righteousness of God in Him.

2 Corinthians 5:20-21

Week 7 NKJV

1 John 5:13

13 These things I have written to you who believe in the name of the Son of God, that you may know that you have eternal life, and that you may continue to believe in the name of the Son of God.

1 John 5:13

Week 10 NKJV

Ephesians 5:1-4

1 Therefore be imitators of God as dear children. 2 And walk in love, as Christ also has loved us and given Himself for us, an offering and a sacrifice to God for a sweet-smelling aroma. 3 But fornication and all uncleanness or covetousness, let it not even be named among you, as is fitting for saints; 4 neither filthiness, nor foolish talking, nor coarse jesting, which are not fitting, but rather giving of thanks.

Ephesians 5:1-4

Week 9 NKJV

Matthew 5:14-16

14 "You are the light of the world. A city that is set on a hill cannot be hidden. 15 Nor do they light a lamp and put it under a basket, but on a lampstand, and it gives light to all who are in the house. 16 Let your light so shine before men, that they may see your good works and glorify your Father in heaven.

Matthew 5:14-16

Week 12 NKJV

Acts 10:38-43

38 how God anointed Jesus of Nazareth with the Holy Spirit and with power, who went about doing good and healing all who were oppressed by the devil, for God was with Him. 39 And we are witnesses of all things which He did both in the land of the Jews and in Jerusalem, whom they killed by hanging on a tree. 40 Him God raised up on the third day, and showed Him openly, 41 not to all the people, but to witnesses chosen before by God, even to us who ate and drank with Him after He arose from the dead. 42 And He commanded us to preach to the people, and to testify that it is He who was ordained by God to be Judge of the living and the dead. 43 To Him all the prophets witness that, through His name, whoever believes in Him will receive remission of sins.

Acts 10:38-43

Week 11 NKJV